ENGLISH
FOR EVERYONE

COURSE BOOK

LEVEL ❷ BEGINNER

FREE AUDIO
website and app
www.dkefe.com

Author

Rachel Harding has a background in English-language teaching and is now a full-time author of English-language learning materials. She has written for major English-language publishers including Oxford University Press.

Course consultant

Tim Bowen has taught English and trained teachers in more than 30 countries worldwide. He is the co-author of works on pronunciation teaching and language-teaching methodology, and author of numerous books for English-language teachers. He is currently a freelance materials writer, editor, and translator. He is a member of the Chartered Institute of Linguists.

Language consultant

Professor Susan Barduhn is an experienced English-language teacher, teacher trainer, and author, who has contributed to numerous publications. In addition to directing English-language courses in at least four different continents, she has been President of the International Association of Teachers of English as a Foreign Language, and an adviser to the British Council and the US State Department. She is currently a Professor at the School for International Training in Vermont, USA.

ENGLISH
FOR EVERYONE

COURSE BOOK

LEVEL 2 BEGINNER

SECOND EDITION
Senior Editor Ankita Awasthi Tröger
Editor Elizabeth Blakemore
Art Editor Amy Child
Managing Editor Carine Tracanelli
Managing Art Editor Anna Hall
Production Editor Gillian Reid
Senior Production Controller Poppy David
Jacket Designer Surabhi Wadhwa-Gandhi
Jacket Design Development Manager Sophia MTT
Publisher Andrew Macintyre
Art Director Karen Self
Publishing Director Jonathan Metcalf

DK INDIA
Senior Jackets Coordinator Priyanka Sharma Saddi
DTP Designer Rakesh Kumar

FIRST EDITION
US Editors Allison Singer, Jenny Siklos
Editors Gareth Clark, Lisa Gillespie, Andrew Kerr-Jarrett
Art Editors Chrissy Barnard, Ray Bryant
Senior Art Editor Sharon Spencer
Editorial Assistants Jessica Cawthra, Sarah Edwards
Illustrators Edwood Burn, Denise Joos, Michael Parkin, Jemma Westing
Audio Producer Liz Hammond
Managing Editor Daniel Mills
Managing Art Editor Anna Hall
Project Manager Christine Stroyan
Producer, Pre-Production Luca Frassinetti
Producer Mary Slater
Jacket Designer Natalie Godwin
Jacket Editor Claire Gell
Jacket Design Development Manager Sophia MTT
Publisher Andrew Macintyre
Art Director Karen Self
Publishing Director Jonathan Metcalf

DK INDIA
Jacket Designer Surabhi Wadhwa
Managing Jackets Editor Saloni Singh
Senior DTP Designer Harish Aggarwal

This American Edition, 2024
First American Edition, 2016
Published in the United States by DK Publishing,
a division of Penguin Random House LLC
1745 Broadway, 20th Floor, New York, NY 10019

This book was made with Forest
Stewardship Council™ certified
paper – one small step in DK's
commitment to a sustainable future.
Learn more at
www.dk.com/uk/information/sustainability

Contents

How the course works   8

01 Talking about yourself   12
New language Using "to be"
Vocabulary Names, jobs, and family
New skill Talking about yourself

02 Talking about routines   16
New language The present simple
Vocabulary Routines and pastimes
New skill Talking about routines

03 Today I'm wearing...   20
New language The present continuous
Vocabulary Clothes and activities
New skill Talking about what's happening now

04 What's happening?   24
New language Present continuous questions
Vocabulary Activities and gadgets
New skill Asking about the present

05 Types of verbs   28
New language Action and state verbs
Vocabulary Activities
New skill Using state verbs

06 Vocabulary Feelings and moods   30

07 How are you feeling? 32
New language "Feeling" and emotions
Vocabulary Adjectives of emotions
New skill Talking about your feelings

08 Vocabulary Transportation 36

09 Routines and exceptions 38
New language Exceptions
Vocabulary Time markers
New skill Contrasting routines and exceptions

10 Vocabulary The body 42

11 What's the matter? 44
New language Health complaints
Vocabulary Body parts and pain phrases
New skill Saying what's wrong

12 Vocabulary Weather 46

13 What's the weather like? 48
New language Weather descriptions
Vocabulary Temperature words
New skill Talking about the weather

14 Vocabulary Travel 52

15 Making comparisons 54
New language Comparative adjectives
Vocabulary Travel and countries
New skill Comparing things

16 Talking about extremes 58
New language Superlative adjectives
Vocabulary Animals, facts, and places
New skill Talking about extremes

17 Vocabulary Geographical features 62

18 Making choices 64
New language "Which" and "what"
Vocabulary Geographical words
New skill Asking multiple-choice questions

19 Using large numbers 68
New language Large numbers
Vocabulary Thousands and millions
New skill Talking about large amounts

20 Vocabulary The calendar 70

21 Talking about dates 72
New language Dates, "was born," "ago"
Vocabulary Numbers, months, and years
New skill Talking about dates

22 Talking about the past 74

New language The past simple of "to be"
Vocabulary Jobs, town, and life events
New skill Talking about past states

23 Past events 78

New language Regular verbs in the past simple
Vocabulary Pastimes and life events
New skill Talking about your past

24 Past abilities 82

New language Using "could" in the past simple
Vocabulary Abilities and pastimes
New skill Talking about past abilities

25 Vocabulary Entertainment 84

26 Irregular past verbs 86

New language Irregular verbs in the past simple
Vocabulary Sequence words
New skill Describing the past

27 Vocabulary Tools and implements 92

28 Telling a story 94

New language "About," opinions
Vocabulary Opinions
New skill Describing media and culture

29 Asking about the past 98

New language Past simple questions
Vocabulary Travel and activities
New skill Talking about vacations

30 Applying for a job 102

New language Interview responses
Vocabulary Job words and phrases
New skill Dealing with job applications

31 Types of questions 104

New language Subject and object questions
Vocabulary Workplace words
New skill Asking different kinds of question

32 Someone, anyone, everyone 108

New language Indefinite pronouns
Vocabulary Office words
New skill Talking about people in general

33 Making conversation 110

New language Short questions
Vocabulary Question words
New skill Asking short questions

34 Vocabulary Going out 112

35 Future arrangements 114

New language Future with present continuous
Vocabulary Excuses
New skill Talking about future arrangements

36 Plans and intentions 118

New language Future tense
Vocabulary Time words and phrases
New skill Talking about your plans

37 What's going to happen 122

New language The future with "going to"
Vocabulary Prediction verbs
New skill Predicting future events

38 Vocabulary Animals 126

39 Making predictions 128

New language The future with "will"
Vocabulary Prediction words
New skill Saying what you think will happen

40 Making quick decisions 132

New language Quick decisions with "will"
Vocabulary Decision words
New skill Talking about future actions

41 Future possibilities 136

New language Using "might"
Vocabulary Activities, food, and pastimes
New skill Talking about future possibilities

42 Giving advice 140

New language "Should"
Vocabulary Advice
New skill Giving advice

43 Making suggestions 144

New language "Could" for suggestions
Vocabulary Advice
New skill Making suggestions

44 Vocabulary Household chores 148

45 Around the house 150

New language The present perfect
Vocabulary Household chores
New skill Talking about the recent past

46 Events in your life 154

New language The present perfect
Vocabulary Adventure sports
New skill Talking about past events

47 Events in your year 158

New language "Yet" and "already"
Vocabulary Routines and chores
New skill Talking about the recent past

48 Eating out 162

New language Restaurant phrases
Vocabulary Food preparation
New skill Ordering a meal in a restaurant

49 Achievements and ambitions 164

New language Desires and plans
Vocabulary Travel and adventure sports
New skill Talking about your achievements

Reference 168

Transcripts of listening exercises 176

Answers 184

Index 197

How the course works

English for Everyone is designed for people who want to teach themselves the English language. Like all language courses, it covers the core skills: grammar, vocabulary, pronunciation, listening, speaking, reading, and writing. Unlike in other courses, the skills are taught and practiced as visually as possible, using images and graphics to help you understand and remember. The best way to learn is to work through the book in order, making full use of the audio available on the website and app. Turn to the practice book at the end of each unit to reinforce your learning with additional exercises.

PRACTICE BOOK

COURSE BOOK

Unit number The book is divided into units. The unit number helps you keep track of your progress.

Learning points Every unit begins with a summary of the key learning points.

Modules Each unit is broken down into modules, which should be done in order. You can take a break from learning after completing any module.

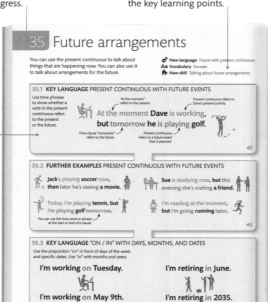

Language learning Modules with colored backgrounds teach new vocabulary and grammar. Study these carefully before moving on to the exercises.

Audio support Most modules have supporting audio recordings of native English speakers to help you improve your speaking and listening skills.

Exercises Modules with white backgrounds contain exercises that help you practice your new skills to reinforce learning.

FREE AUDIO
website and app
www.dkefe.com

Language modules

New language points are taught in carefully graded stages, starting with a simple explanation of when they are used, then offering further examples of common usage, and a detailed breakdown of how key constructions are formed.

Module number Every module is identified with a unique number, so you can track your progress and easily locate any related audio.

Module heading The teaching topic appears here, along with a brief introduction.

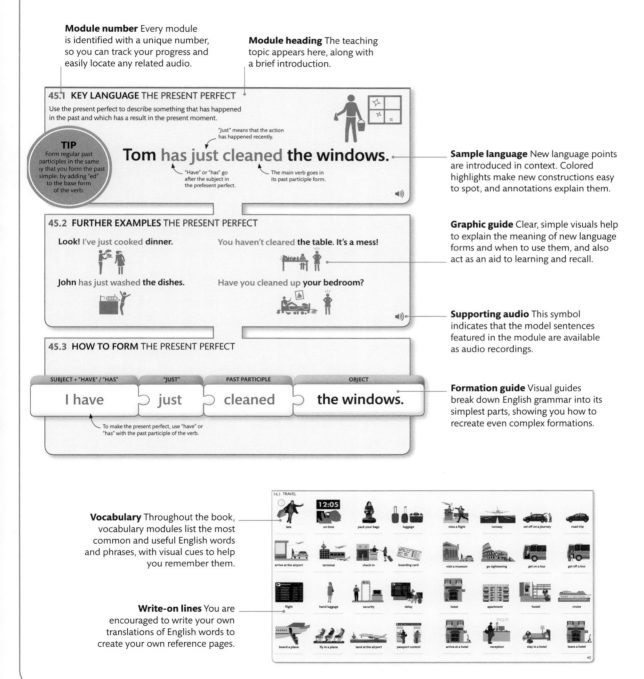

45.1 KEY LANGUAGE THE PRESENT PERFECT

Use the present perfect to describe something that has happened in the past and which has a result in the present moment.

"Just" means that the action has happened recently.

TIP
Form regular past participles in the same way that you form the past simple, by adding "ed" to the base form of the verb.

Tom has just cleaned the windows.

"Have" or "has" go after the subject in the present perfect.

The main verb goes in its past participle form.

Sample language New language points are introduced in context. Colored highlights make new constructions easy to spot, and annotations explain them.

45.2 FURTHER EXAMPLES THE PRESENT PERFECT

Look! I've just cooked **dinner.**

You haven't cleared **the table. It's a mess!**

John has just washed **the dishes.**

Have you cleaned up **your bedroom?**

Graphic guide Clear, simple visuals help to explain the meaning of new language forms and when to use them, and also act as an aid to learning and recall.

Supporting audio This symbol indicates that the model sentences featured in the module are available as audio recordings.

45.3 HOW TO FORM THE PRESENT PERFECT

SUBJECT + "HAVE" / "HAS"	"JUST"	PAST PARTICIPLE	OBJECT
I have	just	cleaned	the windows.

To make the present perfect, use "have" or "has" with the past participle of the verb.

Formation guide Visual guides break down English grammar into its simplest parts, showing you how to recreate even complex formations.

Vocabulary Throughout the book, vocabulary modules list the most common and useful English words and phrases, with visual cues to help you remember them.

Write-on lines You are encouraged to write your own translations of English words to create your own reference pages.

14.1 TRAVEL

late	on time	pack your bags	luggage	miss a flight	runway	set off on a journey	road trip
arrive at the airport	terminal	check-in	boarding card	visit a museum	go sightseeing	get on a bus	get off a bus
flight	hand luggage	security	delay	hotel	apartment	hostel	cruise
board a plane	fly in a plane	land at the airport	passport control	arrive at a hotel	reception	stay in a hotel	leave a hotel

Practice modules

Each exercise is carefully graded to drill and test the language taught in the corresponding course book units. Working through the exercises alongside the course book will help you remember what you have learned and become more fluent. Every exercise is introduced with a symbol to indicate which skill is being practiced.

GRAMMAR
Apply new language rules in different contexts.

READING
Examine target language in real-life English contexts.

LISTENING
Test your understanding of spoken English.

VOCABULARY
Cement your understanding of key vocabulary.

SPEAKING
Compare your spoken English to model audio recordings.

Module number Every module is identified with a unique number, so you can easily locate answers and related audio.

Exercise instruction Every exercise is introduced with a brief instruction, telling you what you need to do.

Sample answer The first question of each exercise is answered for you, to help make the task easy to understand.

Space for writing You are encouraged to write your answers in the book for future reference.

Speaking exercise This symbol indicates that you should say your answers out loud, then compare them to model recordings included in your audio files.

Supporting graphics Visual cues are given to help you understand the exercises.

Supporting audio This symbol shows that the answers to the exercise are available as audio tracks. Listen to them after completing the exercise.

1.5 FILL IN THE GAPS WITH "AM," "IS," OR "ARE"

I _____ am _____ an actor.

1 You _____ British.

2 He _____ a farmer.

3 They _____ 13 years old.

4 We _____ French.

5 I _____ an engineer.

16.12 SAY THE SENTENCES OUT LOUD, FILLING IN THE GAPS USING SUPERLATIVES

Mount Everest is a very high mountain. It is _____ the highest _____ mountain in the world.

1 Istanbul is a very large city. It is _____ city in Europe.

2 The Missouri River is 2,540 miles long. It is _____ river in North America.

3 The cheetah is a very fast animal. It is _____ land animal on Earth.

4 The Kali Gandaki Gorge is 3.46 miles deep. It is _____ gorge in the world.

Listening exercise This symbol indicates that you should listen to an audio track in order to answer the questions in the exercise.

29.4 LISTEN TO THE AUDIO, THEN NUMBER THE PICTURES IN THE ORDER THEY ARE DESCRIBED

Bea talks about her vacation in India.

Audio

English for Everyone features extensive supporting audio materials. You are encouraged to use them as much as you can, to improve your understanding of spoken English, and to make your own accent and pronunciation more natural. Each file can be played, paused, and repeated as often as you like, until you are confident you understand what has been said.

LISTENING EXERCISES
This symbol indicates that you should listen to an audio track in order to answer the questions in the exercise.

SUPPORTING AUDIO
This symbol indicates that extra audio material is available for you to listen to after completing the module.

FREE AUDIO
website and app
www.dkefe.com

Track your progress

The course is designed to make it easy to monitor your progress, with regular summary and review modules. Answers are provided for every exercise, so you can see how well you have understood each teaching point.

Checklists Every unit ends with a checklist, where you can check off the new skills you have learned.

Review modules At the end of a group of units, you will find a more detailed review module, summarizing the language you have learned.

Check boxes Use these boxes to mark the skills you feel comfortable with. Go back and review anything you feel you need to practice further.

Answers Find the answers to every exercise printed at the back of the book.

Exercise numbers Match these numbers to the unique identifier at the top-left corner of each exercise.

Audio This symbol indicates that the answers can also be listened to.

01 Talking about yourself

When you want to tell someone about yourself, or about people and things that relate to you, use the present simple form of "to be."

⚙ **New language** Using "to be"
Aa Vocabulary Names, jobs, and family
🧩 **New skill** Talking about yourself

1.1 KEY LANGUAGE "TO BE" STATEMENTS

Use the verb "to be" to talk about your name, age, nationality, and job.

Hi! I am Noah. I'm 25 years old. I'm Australian and I'm a doctor.

In conversational English, speakers often use contractions. These are shortened versions of pairs of words. "I am" can be shortened to "I'm."

1.2 FURTHER EXAMPLES "TO BE" STATEMENTS

Mia is **72 years old.**

Aban is **a police officer.**

Jack's aunt is **Canadian.**

They are **the Jackson family.**

1.3 HOW TO FORM "TO BE" STATEMENTS

"You" in English is the same in the singular and plural.

These are pronouns. They are the subjects of these sentences.

SUBJECT	"TO BE"	REST OF SENTENCE
I	am	
You	are	
He / She / It	is	Australian.
We / They	are	

The verb changes with the subject.

1.4 CROSS OUT THE INCORRECT WORD IN EACH SENTENCE

They are / ~~is~~ builders.

1. You **are** / **is** 40 years old.
2. I **am** / **is** from New Zealand.

3. He **is** / **are** my cousin.
4. We **am** / **are** British.
5. They **is** / **are** mechanics.

6. She **is** / **are** my sister.
7. We **is** / **are** scientists.
8. She **is** / **are** 21 years old.

1.5 FILL IN THE GAPS WITH "AM," "IS," OR "ARE"

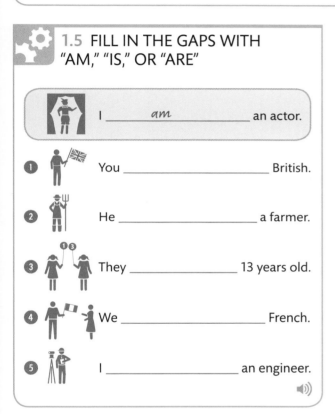

I _____ *am* _____ an actor.

1. You _____ British.
2. He _____ a farmer.
3. They _____ 13 years old.
4. We _____ French.
5. I _____ an engineer.

1.6 LISTEN TO THE AUDIO AND ANSWER THE QUESTIONS

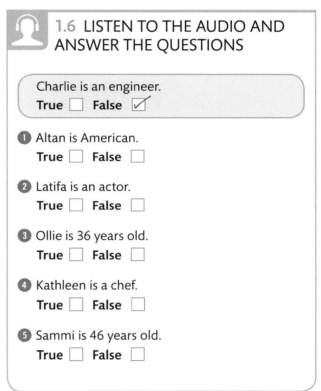

Charlie is an engineer.
True ☐ **False** ☑

1. Altan is American.
True ☐ **False** ☐

2. Latifa is an actor.
True ☐ **False** ☐

3. Ollie is 36 years old.
True ☐ **False** ☐

4. Kathleen is a chef.
True ☐ **False** ☐

5. Sammi is 46 years old.
True ☐ **False** ☐

1.7 USE THE CHART TO CREATE 10 CORRECT SENTENCES, THEN SAY THEM OUT LOUD

I am Jack.

| I / He / They | am / is / are | Jack. / 40 years old. / Canadian. / an engineer. |

Choose a subject. | Choose a verb form. | Finish with a name, age, nationality, or job.

13

1.8 KEY LANGUAGE NEGATIVE "TO BE" STATEMENTS

To make a negative statement, add "not" after the verb.

I am not **a nurse.** I am **a scientist.**

1.9 FURTHER EXAMPLES NEGATIVE "TO BE" STATEMENTS

"Are not" is often contracted to "aren't."

They aren't **Canadian.**

I'm not **happy today.**

"Is not" is often contracted to "isn't."

He isn't **at work this morning.**

Lucy is not **my friend.**

1.10 FILL IN THE GAPS TO MAKE NEGATIVE SENTENCES

It _____*is not*_____ 11 o'clock.

1 He _____ playing tennis.

2 She _____ a waitress.

3 He _____ 30 years old.

4 We _____ teachers.

5 I _____ at work.

6 Lyla _____ a cat.

1.11 WRITE EACH SENTENCE IN ITS NEGATIVE FORM

I am an engineer.

I am not an engineer.

1 Kaleh is their mother.

_____

2 There is a bank on this street.

_____

3 That is his laptop.

_____

4 They are her grandparents.

_____

5 Alyssa and Logan are your friends.

_____

1.12 KEY LANGUAGE "TO BE" QUESTIONS

To ask a "to be" question, put the verb before the subject.

In a statement, the subject comes before the verb.

You are **Canadian.**

Are you **Canadian?**

In a question, the verb moves to the start of the sentence.

The subject comes after the verb.

1.13 FURTHER EXAMPLES "TO BE" QUESTIONS

Is Shia **an actor?**

Are they **engineers?**

Are you **French?**

Is she **a student?**

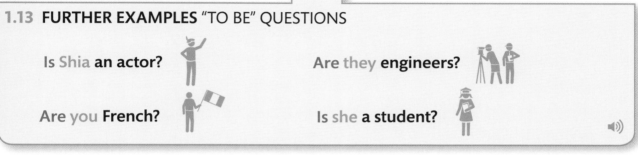

1.14 REWRITE THE SENTENCES AS QUESTIONS

She is a gardener.
Is she a gardener?

1. Alvera is a nurse.

2. Those are my keys.

3. Ruby and Farid are artists.

4. They are best friends.

1.15 SAY THESE QUESTIONS OUT LOUD, FILLING IN THE GAPS

Is _____ she a waitress?

1. _____ Holly your mother?

2. _____ they from Argentina?

3. _____ these your dogs?

4. _____ this Main Street?

02 Talking about routines

You can use present simple statements to describe your daily routines, pastimes, and possessions. Use "do" to form negatives and ask questions.

🔧 **New language** The present simple
Aa Vocabulary Routines and pastimes
🧩 **New skill** Talking about routines

2.1 KEY LANGUAGE THE PRESENT SIMPLE

To make the present simple, use the base form of the verb (the infinitive without "to").

This is the base form of the verb "to eat."

I eat lunch at 12 o'clock every day.

She eats lunch at 1:30pm every day.

With "he," "she," and "it," add "s" to the base form.

2.2 FURTHER EXAMPLES THE PRESENT SIMPLE

They go to the gym at 8am.

Jamal goes to the gym at 9am.

Verbs ending "sh," "ch," "o," "ss," "x," and "z" take "es" in the third person singular.

I have a microwave.

She has a dog and a cat.

The verb "have" is irregular. Use "has" for "he," "she," and "it."

2.3 HOW TO FORM THE PRESENT SIMPLE

SUBJECT	VERB	REST OF SENTENCE
I / You / We / They	eat	lunch at 1pm every day.
He / She	eats	

With "he," "she," and "it," add "s."

2.4 CROSS OUT THE INCORRECT WORD IN EACH SENTENCE

She ~~eat~~ / eats dinner in the evening.

1 He wake up / wakes up at 7 o'clock.

2 I start / starts work at 10am.

3 They leave / leaves home at 8:45am.

4 We finish / finishes work at 4pm.

5 My friend has / have dinner at 6:30pm.

6 I cook / cooks dinner every night.

7 My parents eat / eats lunch at 2pm.

8 Mia get / gets up at 5 o'clock.

9 My cousin work / works with animals.

2.5 FILL IN THE GAPS USING THE WORDS IN THE PANEL

 Michael ___*gets up*___ at 7:30am.

1 We _____ work at 5:30pm.

2 Pam _____ lunch at 1:30pm.

3 We _____ in the park.

4 His son _____ work at 9am.

5 My brother _____ work at 4:45pm.

6 They _____ dinner at 8pm.

~~gets up~~   walk   goes to

leaves   eat   eats   leave

2.6 SAY THE SENTENCES OUT LOUD, FILLING IN THE GAPS

Sonia _____*goes*_____ (go) to work early.

1 My son _____ (watch) TV all night.

2 He _____ (go) shopping on Fridays.

3 We _____ (eat) breakfast at 7am.

4 My cousin _____ (work) inside.

5 Georgia _____ (start) work at 9am.

6 They _____ (do) their chores.

2.7 KEY LANGUAGE THE PRESENT SIMPLE NEGATIVE

Use "do not" before the main verb to make the negative. If the subject is "he," "she," or "it," use "does not."

The main verb does not change.

I do not work outside.
I work inside.

He does not work inside.
He works outside.

2.8 FURTHER EXAMPLES THE PRESENT SIMPLE NEGATIVE

You can contract "do not" to "don't" and "does not" to "doesn't."

 He does not live in France.

 This house doesn't have a yard.

2.9 HOW TO FORM THE PRESENT SIMPLE NEGATIVE

SUBJECT	"DO / DOES" + NOT	VERB BASE FORM	REST OF SENTENCE
I / You / We / They	do not	work	outside.
He / She / It	does not		

2.10 FILL IN THE GAPS TO WRITE EACH SENTENCE THREE DIFFERENT WAYS

He gets up at 5am.	He does not get up at 5am.	He doesn't get up at 5am.
❶		I don't go to work every day.
❷	He does not watch TV in the evening.	
❸ They work in an office.		

2.11 KEY LANGUAGE QUESTIONS WITH "DO" AND "DOES"

For most verbs other than "to be," add "do"
or "does" to turn a statement into a question.

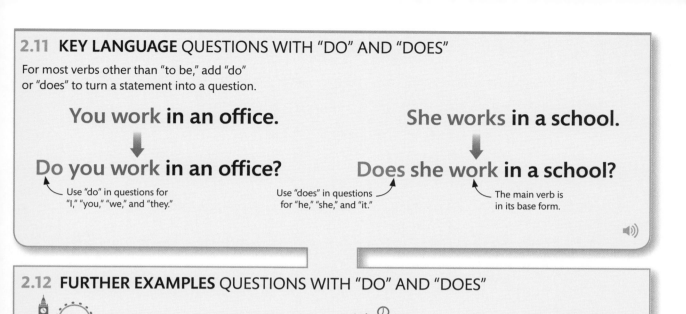

You work **in an office.**

Do you work **in an office?**

Use "do" in questions for
"I," "you," "we," and "they."

Use "does" in questions
for "he," "she," and "it."

She works **in a school.**

Does she work **in a school?**

The main verb is
in its base form.

2.12 FURTHER EXAMPLES QUESTIONS WITH "DO" AND "DOES"

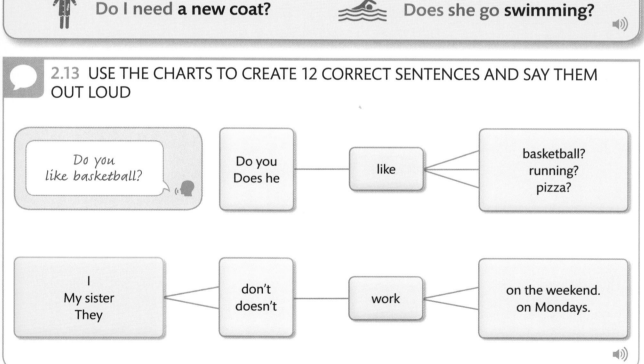

Do they live **in London?**

Do I need **a new coat?**

Does Tom get up **at 7am?**

Does she go **swimming?**

2.13 USE THE CHARTS TO CREATE 12 CORRECT SENTENCES AND SAY THEM OUT LOUD

Do you like basketball?

| Do you Does he | like | basketball? running? pizza? |

| I My sister They | don't doesn't | work | on the weekend. on Mondays. |

03 Today I'm wearing...

You can use the present continuous to describe something that is happening now. It is often used to describe what people are wearing, using, or doing.

🔧 **New language** The present continuous
Aa Vocabulary Clothes and activities
🧩 **New skill** Talking about what's happening now

3.1 KEY LANGUAGE THE PRESENT CONTINUOUS

Use the present continuous form to describe what is happening right now.

This is the present simple. It describes a regular action.

Julie doesn't usually wear dresses, but today she is wearing a bright red dress.

This is the present continuous. It describes what is happening right now.

🔊

3.2 HOW TO FORM THE PRESENT CONTINUOUS

Use "to be" plus the present participle (this is the "-ing" form of the verb) to form the present continuous.

SUBJECT	"TO BE"	VERB + "-ING"	REST OF SENTENCE
She	**is**	**wearing**	**a red dress.**

This is the present participle. These follow the same spelling rules as gerunds.

3.3 FURTHER EXAMPLES THE PRESENT CONTINUOUS

Remember, you can use contractions.

 She is walking **the dog.**

 They're fighting **with each other.**

 He is washing **the dishes.**

 She is relaxing **at the moment.**

We are using **our phones.**

For verbs ending in "e" (such as "use"), take off the "e" and add "ing."

 I am cutting **some apples.**

For single-syllable words ending consonant-vowel-consonant, double the final letter before adding "ing."

 🔊

3.4 CROSS OUT THE INCORRECT WORDS IN THE SENTENCES

They i̶s̶ / are wearing hats.

1 Sharon is / are reading a book.

2 I am / is carrying my laptop.

3 My cat is / are climbing a tree.

4 We is / are working at the moment.

5 They is / are having their dinner.

6 He is / are talking to his dad.

7 I am / are driving to work right now.

8 They am / are watching the movie.

 3.5 FILL IN THE GAPS TO COMPLETE THE SENTENCES

She ___is sleeping___ (sleep) in her bed.

1 They _____ (come) home now.

2 We _____ (play) a board game.

3 Jane _____ (cook) dinner.

4 He _____ (drink) some water.

5 We _____ (listen) to music.

6 I _____ (wash) my hair.

7 You _____ (win) the game.

8 We _____ (visit) New Zealand.

 3.6 LISTEN TO THE AUDIO AND MATCH THE PORTRAITS TO THE NAMES

| Emma | Emma's dad | Julie | Max | Emma's cousin |

3.7 KEY LANGUAGE THE PRESENT CONTINUOUS NEGATIVE

Make the negative of the present continuous by adding "not" after "to be." Don't change the present participle.

He is wearing **a tie, but** he $\left\{ \begin{array}{c} \text{is not} \\ \text{isn't} \end{array} \right\}$ wearing **a hat.**

Add "not" after "to be" to make the negative. You can use contractions, too.

You still use the present participle when you make the negative.

3.8 HOW TO FORM THE PRESENT CONTINUOUS NEGATIVE

SUBJECT	NEGATIVE + "TO BE"	VERB + "-ING"	REST OF SENTENCE
He	isn't	wearing	a hat.

Use the present participle.

3.9 FURTHER EXAMPLES THE PRESENT CONTINUOUS NEGATIVE

 She isn't walking **the dog.**   We aren't taking **the bus today.**

They aren't singing **well today.**   You aren't doing **your job!**

3.10 CROSS OUT THE INCORRECT WORDS IN THE SENTENCES

They ~~isn't~~ / aren't wearing coats.

1 We isn't / **aren't** playing with them.

2 The baby **isn't** / aren't sleeping.

3 He **isn't** / aren't watching the game.

4 You isn't / **aren't** wearing boots.

5 She **isn't** / aren't cooking lunch.

6 We isn't / **aren't** meeting right now.

7 I am not / aren't eating with them.

3.11 FILL IN THE GAPS WITH THE PRESENT CONTINUOUS NEGATIVE

Sheila _isn't walking_ (walk) the dog.

1 They _____ (go) to the park.

2 I _____ (eat) this meal.

3 You _____ (wear) this coat again.

4 Frank's dog _____ (sit) by the fire.

5 My dad _____ (carry) the heavy box.

🔊

3.12 LISTEN TO THE AUDIO AND MARK THE CORRECT ACTIVITIES

Ed's watching TV. ☐
Ed's reading. ☑

1 Dan is sleeping. ☐
Dan's watching a movie. ☐

2 Manu is dancing. ☐
Manu's exercising. ☐

3 George's playing his guitar. ☐
George is singing. ☐

4 Jamal is walking the dog. ☐
Jamal is playing a computer game. ☐

3.13 SAY POSITIVE AND NEGATIVE SENTENCES BASED ON THE IMAGES

They are running.
They aren't running.

1

2

3

🔊

04 What's happening?

You can use the present continuous to ask about things that are happening now, at the time of speaking.

⚙ **New language** Present continuous questions
Aa Vocabulary Activities and gadgets
🧩 **New skill** Asking about the present

4.1 KEY LANGUAGE PRESENT CONTINUOUS QUESTIONS

Use present continuous questions to ask about what is happening now.

"He" is the subject.

What is he doing?

He is playing tennis.

This action is taking place now.

4.2 HOW TO FORM PRESENT CONTINUOUS QUESTIONS

To make a question in the present continuous, swap the subject and "to be." You can also add question words.

QUESTION WORD	"TO BE"	SUBJECT	VERB + "-ING"
What	is	he	doing?

4.3 FURTHER EXAMPLES PRESENT CONTINUOUS QUESTIONS

Where are they going?

Who is he working with?

What are you eating?

Why is she running?

4.4 VOCABULARY COMMON PRESENT CONTINUOUS VERBS

hold

carry

clean

use

4.5 LISTEN TO THE AUDIO AND WRITE WHO'S DOING EACH ACTIVITY

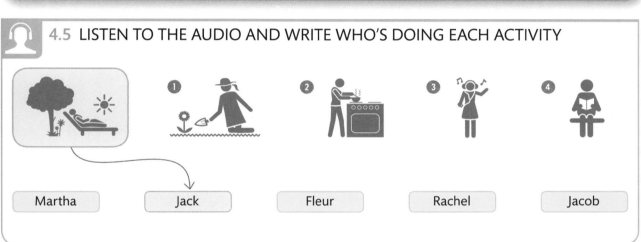

Martha

Jack

Fleur

Rachel

Jacob

Aa 4.6 MATCH THE QUESTIONS TO THE ANSWERS

What is Jim doing?

They are eating chocolate.

① What are John and Mike watching?

She is singing "Happy Birthday."

② What is Sida singing?

They are cooking dinner.

③ Where are you going?

He is reading a book.

④ What are Anna and Sue eating?

They are watching a movie.

⑤ What are Ali and Sam doing?

We are going to the store.

25

4.7 VOCABULARY DIGITAL GADGETS

tablet   computer   smartphone   games console   headphones   e-reader

4.8 FILL IN THE GAPS USING THE PRESENT CONTINUOUS

Jack is ___*holding*___ his tablet.

1. Sam is _____ red pants.

2. Jack is _____ on an e-reader.

3. You are _____ to headphones.

4. Sam is _____ her bike.

5. I am _____ my smartphone.

| reading | cleaning | using |
| listening | ~~holding~~ | wearing |

4.9 LISTEN TO THE AUDIO, ANSWER THE QUESTIONS

What is Jim holding?
an e-reader ☐   a smartphone ✓

1. What is Lucas cleaning?
his shirt ☐   his shoes ☐

2. What is Orla using?
a computer ☐   a games console ☐

3. What is Livia wearing?
a skirt ☐   a dress ☐

4. What is David doing right now?
writing ☐   reading ☐

5. What is Dewain listening to?
some music ☐   the radio ☐

6. What is Rochelle carrying?
her tablet ☐   her laptop ☐

7. What is Julio using?
his tablet ☐   his e-reader ☐

4.10 REWRITE THE QUESTIONS, CORRECTING THE ERRORS

Where Lill is going?
Where is Lill going?

① What cleaning is Kimi?
_____

② What is doing Jill?
_____

③ Using what is Jack?
_____

④ Max what is holding?
_____

⑤ Is what carrying Marge?
_____

4.11 LOOK AT THE PICTURES AND ANSWER THE QUESTIONS, SPEAKING OUT LOUD

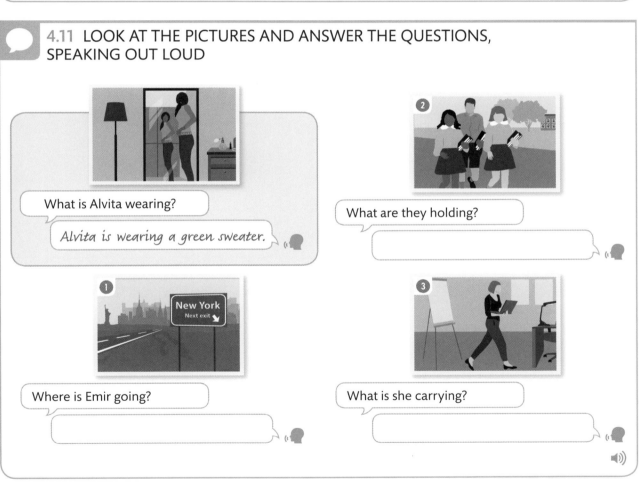

What is Alvita wearing?

Alvita is wearing a green sweater.

What are they holding?

Where is Emir going?

What is she carrying?

05 Types of verbs

You can use most verbs in the continuous form to describe ongoing actions. Some verbs cannot be used in this way. These are called "state" verbs.

⚙ **New language** Action and state verbs
Aa Vocabulary Activities
🧩 **New skill** Using state verbs

5.1 KEY LANGUAGE ACTION AND STATE VERBS

Action verbs usually describe what people or things do. State verbs usually say how things are or how someone feels.

ACTION VERB

I { read / am reading } a book.

Action verbs can be used in simple forms and continuous forms.

STATE VERB

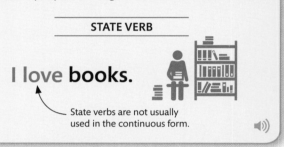

I love **books.**

State verbs are not usually used in the continuous form.

5.2 FURTHER EXAMPLES ACTION AND STATE VERBS

Dominic is eating **ice cream.**

Gayle is lying **on the couch.**

I want **to go on vacation.**

She has **two cats and a dog.**

Aa 5.3 FIND EIGHT VERBS IN THE GRID AND WRITE THEM UNDER THE CORRECT HEADING

```
L O V E B I R A C S A H
T P Q A Y H E N V T Q A
R E M E M B E R D H M T
W A N T L E R E A D T E
L T B C O W D K S V X C
E E D E V T W E E E A I
L E A R N L A O E R G O
```

ACTION VERBS:

1 _____
2 _____
3 _____
4 _____

STATE VERBS:

1 _____want_____
2 _____
3 _____
4 _____

5.4 ⚠ COMMON MISTAKES STATE VERBS

It is incorrect to use state verbs in the continuous form.

I want a new laptop. ✓

You can usually only use
state verbs in the simple form.

I am wanting a new laptop. ✗

You can't usually use state verbs
in the continuous form.

5.5 REWRITE THE SENTENCES, CORRECTING THE ERRORS

> He is liking the book.
> *He likes the book.*

❶ I am having a big house by the ocean.

_____

❷ My sister is hating this new TV show.

_____

❸ Thomas is knowing your dad.

_____

❹ Finn is wanting a new bike.

_____

❺ I am seeing the cat and dog.

_____

5.6 CROSS OUT THE INCORRECT WORDS IN THE SENTENCES

I want / am wanting some chocolate.

❶ She goes / is going to the store now.

❷ Fred doesn't like / isn't liking pizza.

❸ I always sing / am singing in the bath.

❹ He reads / is reading a book at the moment.

❺ Jo remembers / 's remembering my birthday.

❻ Li plays / is playing tennis at the moment.

❼ We don't want / are not wanting to leave.

---

05 ✓ **CHECKLIST**

⚙ Action and state verbs ☐   **Aa** Activities ☐   🧩 Using state verbs ☐

6.1 FEELINGS AND MOODS

calm

relaxed

happy

confident

proud

excited

surprised

pleased

cheerful

amused

irritated

angry

annoyed

furious

sad

unhappy

worried

lonely

scared

terrified

nervous

anxious

distracted

confused

disappointed

miserable

stressed

jealous

tired

bored

curious

grateful

31

07 How are you feeling?

Talking about your feelings is an important part of everyday conversation. Use the present continuous to talk about how you're feeling.

⚙ **New language** "Feeling" and emotions
Aa Vocabulary Adjectives of emotions
🧩 **New skill** Talking about your feelings

TIP
"Feel" is a sta[?] verb that ca[?] be used in continuous forms.

7.1 KEY LANGUAGE TALKING ABOUT YOUR FEELINGS

You can use the verb "to be" plus "feeling" to talk about your feelings.

How are you **feeling?**
Use "how" as the question word.

I am feeling happy.
You can use different adjectives to describe your feelings.

🔊

7.2 HOW TO FORM TALKING ABOUT YOUR FEELINGS

SUBJECT + "TO BE"	"FEELING"	FEELING ADJECTIVE
I am	**feeling**	**happy.**

Use the verb "to be."

The adjective comes at the end of the sentence.

7.3 FURTHER EXAMPLES TALKING ABOUT YOUR FEELINGS

 I'm **feeling happy.**

 He is **feeling angry.**

 You are **feeling proud.**

 She is **feeling excited.**

 I am **feeling sad.**

 He's **feeling scared.**

🔊

Aa 7.4 MATCH THE FEELINGS TO THEIR OPPOSITES

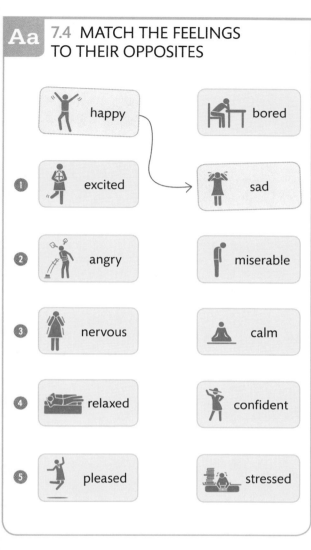

happy

bored

① excited

sad

② angry

miserable

③ nervous

calm

④ relaxed

confident

⑤ pleased

stressed

⚙ 7.5 FILL IN THE GAPS TO COMPLETE THE SENTENCES

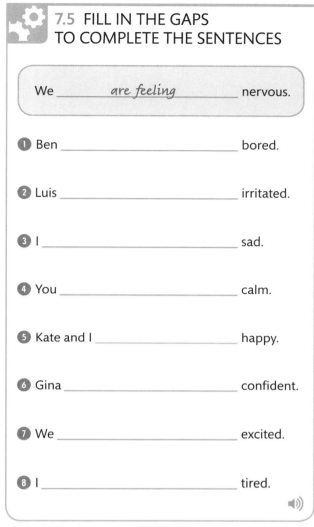

We ___*are feeling*___ nervous.

① Ben _____ bored.

② Luis _____ irritated.

③ I _____ sad.

④ You _____ calm.

⑤ Kate and I _____ happy.

⑥ Gina _____ confident.

⑦ We _____ excited.

⑧ I _____ tired.

🎧 7.6 LISTEN TO THE AUDIO AND ANSWER THE QUESTIONS

Jack is feeling confident.
True ☐ **False** ☑

① Jill is feeling happy.
True ☐ **False** ☐

② Sami is feeling nervous.
True ☐ **False** ☐

③ Ian is feeling bored.
True ☐ **False** ☐

④ Lindi is feeling annoyed.
True ☐ **False** ☐

⑤ Jenny is feeling happy.
True ☐ **False** ☐

⑥ Jimmi is feeling excited.
True ☐ **False** ☐

⑦ Minna is feeling scared.
True ☐ **False** ☐

⑧ Aziz is feeling tired.
True ☐ **False** ☐

7.7 ANOTHER WAY TO SAY IT TALKING ABOUT YOUR FEELINGS

You can also ask how someone is, without using "feeling."

How are you?

Ask the question without using the word "feeling."

I'm really happy.

You can show how happy you are by using an adverb before the adjective.

7.8 HOW TO FORM TALKING ABOUT YOUR FEELINGS

SUBJECT + "TO BE"	ADVERB	FEELING ADJECTIVE
I'm	very really so	happy.

Use the subject and the verb "to be."

Place these adverbs before the adjective to emphasize the strength of your feeling.

7.9 FURTHER EXAMPLES TALKING ABOUT YOUR FEELINGS

 I'm **really** angry.

 They're **so** sad.

 You're **very** excited.

 I'm **so** bored.

7.10 REWRITE THE SENTENCES, ADDING ADVERBS

I am excited. (really)
I am really excited.

❶ Joe's unhappy. (very)
_____

❷ Bella and Edith are sad. (really)
_____

❸ Lin is nervous. (very)
_____

❹ She is confident. (very)
_____

❺ They're tired. (so)
_____

I'm having a great day at the beach. All my friends are here and we're playing volleyball. I'm really ___*happy*___ .

1 I'm at the airport. I'm waiting for the flight. I don't have a book. There's nothing to do. I'm really _____ .

2 I'm watching a movie on TV. It's a love story. The man and his wife are in different countries. They're very _____ .

3 We're at the concert. We're waiting for my favorite band in the world to come on stage. We're at the front. I'm so _____ .

4 I'm at the supermarket. There's no milk, no butter, no flour, and no sugar. All the things that I need for the cake. I'm so _____ .

5 I'm waiting to meet my new boss. She's talking to everyone in the office. I don't know what to say to her. I'm very _____ .

| sad | ~~happy~~ | bored | angry | excited | nervous |

8.1 TRANSPORTATION

car

taxi

bus

coach

plane

train

tram

motorcycle (US)
motorbike (UK)

bicycle

boat

yacht

ship

helicopter

bus stop

train station

taxi rank

airport

port

road

railroad tracks (US)
railway line (UK)

walk

ride a bike

fly a plane

drive a car

ticket

fare

steering wheel

tires (US)
tyres (UK)

trunk (US)
boot (UK)

hood (US)
bonnet (UK)

engine

headlights

wheels

09 Routines and exceptions

Use the present simple to describe routines, and the present continuous to say what you are doing now. These tenses are often used together.

⚙ **New language** Exceptions
Aa Vocabulary Time markers
🧩 **New skill** Contrasting routines and exceptions

9.1 KEY LANGUAGE CONTRASTING ROUTINES AND EXCEPTIONS

You can contrast a routine action with an exception to that routine by using "but."

The present simple describes something you do regularly.

This is a time marker.

I usually drive to work, but today I'm walking.

Adverbs of frequency help to show the present simple action is a routine.

Use "but" to contrast the actions.

The present continuous describes something you are doing now.

🔊

9.2 HOW TO FORM CONTRASTING ROUTINES AND EXCEPTIONS

SUBJECT	ADVERB OF FREQUENCY	VERB	"BUT"	TIME MARKER	PRESENT CONTINUOUS
I	usually mostly often	drive,	but	right now today tonight	I'm walking.

9.3 FURTHER EXAMPLES CONTRASTING ROUTINES AND EXCEPTIONS

I often stay **at home on the weekends, but** today I'm shopping **in town.**

They usually go **to the gym after work, but** tonight they're going **to the movies.**

Tonight, we're celebrating **my birthday, but** normally we don't eat **out.**

You can put the exception first.

🔊

9.4 FILL IN THE GAPS BY PUTTING THE VERBS IN THE CORRECT TENSES

Ben usually __sings__ (sing) in the school band, but today he __is playing__ (play) the guitar.

❶ Sarah and I normally _____ (play) tennis on Wednesdays, but today we _____ (swim).

❷ Today, I _____ (have) soup for lunch, but I usually _____ (have) a sandwich.

❸ We often _____ (watch) TV in the evenings, but tonight we _____ (have) a party.

❹ Ben and Tom usually _____ (work) until 6pm, but tonight they _____ (work) until 9pm.

❺ Melanie _____ (ski) in France this winter, but she normally _____ (go) to Italy.

❻ Today, you _____ (drink) water, but you often _____ (have) coffee after lunch.

🔊

9.5 VOCABULARY TIME MARKERS

At the moment, **I'm knitting.**

....

I'm leaving right now.

....

I'm in a meeting this morning.

....

This afternoon, **we're shopping.**

....

Today, **I'm on vacation.**

....

They're seeing a play tonight.

....

9.6 READ THE MESSAGES AND FILL THE GAPS USING THE PRESENT CONTINUOUS

Chrissy _____*is watching a movie*_____.

Chrissy Hi everyone! I'm not studying this evening. I'm watching a movie with friends. What are you up to?

Denzel Hi! I'm seeing a show tonight. Selma was supposed to come too, but she's doing her project instead.

Marlow Hey! I'm playing hockey in the park at the moment. Can you come and play, Roxy? How about you, Rainey?

Roxy Sorry Marlow, I can't play hockey because I'm making dinner for my parents right now.

Teenie Rainey is eating with friends tonight, Marlow. But I'm bringing my hockey kit to the park right now.

Malala I'm having coffee at the moment. Altan is taking a break from work, so he's here too.

❶ Denzel _____.

❷ Selma _____.

❸ Marlow _____.

❹ Roxy _____.

❹ Rainey _____.

❻ Malala _____.

❼ Altan _____.

9.7 LISTEN TO THE AUDIO AND MARK WHICH ACTIVITIES ARE EXCEPTIONS

Ⓐ ☐   Ⓑ ☐   Ⓒ ☑

❶

Ⓐ ☐   Ⓑ ☐   Ⓒ ☐

❷

Ⓐ ☐   Ⓑ ☐   Ⓒ ☐

❸

Ⓐ ☐   Ⓑ ☐   Ⓒ ☐

9.8 SAY THE SENTENCES OUT LOUD, PUTTING THE VERBS IN THE CORRECT TENSES

Phil usually ___runs___ (run), but today ___he is cycling___ (cycle).

① Sally usually_____ (swim), but right now _____ (play) soccer.

② Abe normally _____ (read), but tonight _____ (listen) to music.

③ They often _____ (play) golf, but today _____ (play) hockey.

④ I usually _____ (take) a shower, but today _____ (take) a bath.

09 ✓ CHECKLIST

⚙ Exceptions ☐   Aa Time markers ☐   🧩 Contrasting routines and exceptions ☐

↻ REVIEW THE ENGLISH YOU HAVE LEARNED IN UNITS 01–09

NEW LANGUAGE	SAMPLE SENTENCE	☑	UNIT
TALKING ABOUT YOURSELF AND YOUR DAILY ROUTINE	I am Noah. I'm 25 years old. I eat lunch at 1pm every day.	☐	1.1, 2.1
THE PRESENT CONTINUOUS	She is wearing a red dress.	☐	3.1
PRESENT CONTINUOUS QUESTIONS	What is he doing?	☐	4.1
ACTION AND STATE VERBS	I am reading a book. I love books.	☐	5.1
TALKING ABOUT YOUR FEELINGS	How are you feeling? I am feeling happy.	☐	7.1
ROUTINES AND EXCEPTIONS	I usually drive to work, but today I'm walking.	☐	9.1

10 Vocabulary

10.1 THE BODY

head

hair

face

neck

cheek

chin

shoulders

ear

eye

eyebrow

eyelashes

nose

mouth

lips

teeth

tooth

chest

stomach

arm

hand

fingers

thumb

knuckles

fingernail

leg

thigh

knee

shin

foot

toes

ankle

heel

43

11 What's the matter?

There are many different ways to say you're sick. You often use the negative, "not well," to talk about general illness, and "hurts," "ache," or "pain" for specific problems.

⚙ **New language** Health complaints
Aa Vocabulary Body parts and pain phrases
🧩 **New skill** Saying what's wrong

11.1 KEY LANGUAGE SAYING YOU'RE NOT FEELING WELL

To say what's wrong, use the verb "to be" with "well," "sick," or "ill." You can also use "to be" with "feeling" and an adverb to show the problem continues and to explain how bad it is.

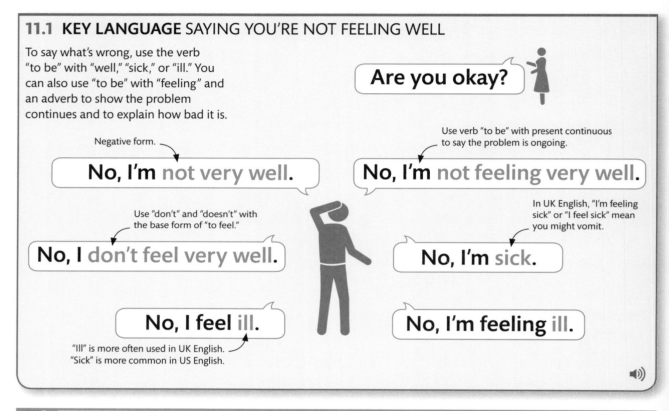

Are you okay?

Negative form.

No, I'm not very well.

Use verb "to be" with present continuous to say the problem is ongoing.

No, I'm not feeling very well.

Use "don't" and "doesn't" with the base form of "to feel."

No, I don't feel very well.

In UK English, "I'm feeling sick" or "I feel sick" mean you might vomit.

No, I'm sick.

No, I feel ill.

"Ill" is more often used in UK English. "Sick" is more common in US English.

No, I'm feeling ill.

11.2 REWRITE THE SENTENCES CORRECTING THE ERRORS

Hilary not feeling well. She's at the doctor.
Hilary's not feeling well. She's at the doctor.

① My brother isn't **feel** very well this morning.

_____

② George **are** sick, so he's staying in bed today.

_____

③ I **is** sick, so I'm not going to work.

_____

④ Ayshah **doesn't** feeling well, so she's going home.

_____

⑤ Luca and Ben **isn't** feeling well today.

_____

11.3 KEY LANGUAGE HEALTH PROBLEMS

Use "have" and "has" with "ache," "pain," and "broken" to say what's wrong. You can also say which part of the body "hurts."

Use "have" with "broken."

I have a broken foot.
My foot hurts.

Use a part of the body with "hurts" to say where the pain is.

Use "in" with "pain" to say where it hurts.

I have a pain in my head.
I have a headache.

Headache is one word.

11.4 FURTHER EXAMPLES HEALTH PROBLEMS

She has a stomach ache.

Susan's leg hurts.

You can use "got" in UK English to say what is wrong.

I've got a broken arm.

Jo has a pain in her back.

Aa 11.5 FILL IN THE GAPS USING THE WORDS IN THE PANEL

I have a bad ____headache____ .

1. Mary's back _____ .

2. John has a _____ leg.

3. I've got a _____ in my finger.

4. She has a terrible _____ .

~~headache~~   toothache   pain   broken   hurts

11.6 MARK THE SENTENCES THAT ARE CORRECT

She has a broken leg. ☑
She have a broken leg. ☐

1. I have a pain in my arm. ☐
   I am a pain in my arm. ☐

2. John has got an earache. ☐
   John has got a earache. ☐

3. He has a head hurt. ☐
   His head hurts. ☐

4. Aziz has got a pain in his back. ☐
   Aziz has got a pain on his back. ☐

11 ✓ CHECKLIST

⚙ Health complaints ☐   **Aa** Body parts and pain phrases ☐   🧩 Saying what's wrong ☐

12.1 WEATHER

cloud

fog

ice

snow

frost

sun

drizzle

rain

hail

wind

gale

storm

thunder

lightning

hurricane/
typhoon/cyclone

tornado

flood

dry

wet

humidity

temperature

warm

hot

boiling

cold

freezing

rainbow

puddle

gray sky (US)
grey sky (UK)

blue sky

12.2 WEATHER ADJECTIVES

sun	→	sunny
cloud	→	cloudy
fog	→	foggy
rain	→	rainy
snow	→	snowy
ice	→	icy
frost	→	frosty
wind	→	windy
storm	→	stormy
thunder	→	thundery

13 What's the weather like?

There are many ways to talk about the weather.
Use the verb "to be" with weather words and phrases
to describe the temperature and conditions.

⚙ **New language** Weather descriptions
Aa Vocabulary Temperature words
New skill Talking about the weather

13.1 KEY LANGUAGE TALKING ABOUT THE WEATHER

To ask about the weather, say: "What's the weather like?" To answer, use the verb "to be" with the correct weather word or phrase.

"Like" is a preposition here, not a verb as it is in "I like music."

What's the weather like?

Okay, but there are a lot of clouds. It's cloudy.

Use "a lot of" with a noun to show the amount of cloud.

13.2 FURTHER EXAMPLES TALKING ABOUT THE WEATHER

Beautiful! It's really hot and sunny.

Horrible! It's raining. It's wet and cold.

Use the present continuous to say what is happening with the weather now.

Really cold. It's snowing a lot and it's very icy.

There's a storm coming. It's very windy.

Aa 13.3 MATCH THE PICTURES TO THE CORRECT SENTENCES

This is a beautiful place, but I really want it to be sunny. It's dark and cloudy all the time.

1

The weather's good, and it's windy today, so we're going sailing with Sue and Louis.

2

The weather is beautiful here. It's hot and sunny, and I'm having a great time.

3

There's a lot of snow, so the children are having a great time. They want to learn how to ski.

🔊

Aa 13.4 FILL IN THE GAPS USING THE WORDS IN THE PANEL

 The weather's lovely here in San Diego. It's really ___*sunny*___ .

1 Oh no! I hate this weather. It's _____ again.

2 I can't ride my bike in these conditions. It's too _____ .

3 Be careful! There's _____ on the road.

4 Wow! It's really _____ outside today.

raining

ice

~~sunny~~

stormy

foggy

🔊

49

13.5 KEY LANGUAGE THE TEMPERATURE

Temperature can be given in "Fahrenheit (°F)" or "Celsius (°C)." In spoken English, use the verb "to be" with a temperature phrase to talk about how hot or cold it is.

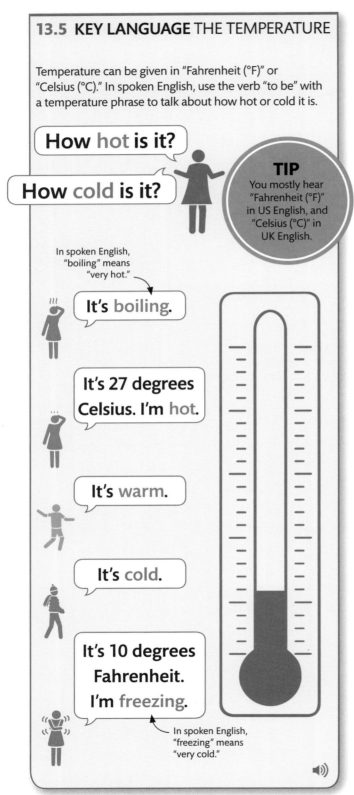

How hot is it?

How cold is it?

TIP
You mostly hear "Fahrenheit (°F)" in US English, and "Celsius (°C)" in UK English.

In spoken English, "boiling" means "very hot."

It's boiling.

It's 27 degrees Celsius. I'm hot.

It's warm.

It's cold.

It's 10 degrees Fahrenheit. I'm freezing.

In spoken English, "freezing" means "very cold."

13.6 READ THE CLUES AND WRITE THE ANSWERS IN THE CORRECT PLACES ON THE GRID

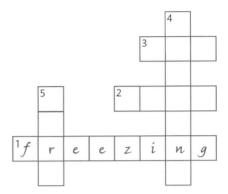

¹ f r e e z i n g

ACROSS

1 It's very cold outside. The temperature is 5°F at the moment, and I'm ___freezing___ .

2 I'm really _____ . Can we have the heating on tonight?

3 Sandra says it's _____ in France today. It's more than 85°F.

DOWN

4 The sun is out and it's 115°F in Turkey today. It's _____ .

5 It's _____ outside today. Everyone's wearing T-shirts.

freezing   hot   warm
    boiling   cold

13.7 LISTEN TO THE AUDIO AND ANSWER THE QUESTIONS

A radio presenter describes the weather across North America.

Where is it 72 degrees Fahrenheit?
Kansas ☐ Boston ☐ Denver ☑

❶ What is the temperature in Calgary?
52°F ☐ 55°F ☐ 60°F ☐

❷ Where is there a storm at the moment?
San Francisco ☐ Seattle ☐ Portland ☐

❸ Where is there snow today?
Vancouver ☐ Edmonton ☐ Anchorage ☐

❹ Where are there no clouds?
Phoenix ☐ Houston ☐ Dallas ☐

13.8 WRITE EACH SENTENCE IN ITS OTHER FORM

There's a lot of fog.
It's very foggy.

❶ It's very icy.
_____

❷ There's a lot of wind.
_____

❸ There's a lot of rain.
_____

❹ The sun is shining.
_____

❺ It's very cloudy.
_____

13 ✅ CHECKLIST

⚙ Weather descriptions ☐   **Aa** Temperature words ☐   🧩 Talking about the weather ☐

🔄 REVIEW THE ENGLISH YOU HAVE LEARNED IN UNITS 11-13

NEW LANGUAGE	SAMPLE SENTENCE	☑	UNIT
SAYING YOU'RE NOT FEELING WELL	**Are you okay? No, I'm** not feeling very well.	☐	11.1
HEALTH PROBLEMS	**I have a** broken foot. **My foot** hurts. **I have a** pain **in my head. I have a** headache.	☐	11.3, 11.4
TALKING ABOUT THE WEATHER	**What's the weather like? Okay, but there are** a lot of clouds. **It's** cloudy.	☐	13.1, 13.2
GIVING THE TEMPERATURE	It's 27 degrees Celsius. It's 10 degrees Fahrenheit.	☐	13.5
TEMPERATURE PHRASES	**How hot is it? It's** boiling. **How cold is it? It's** freezing.	☐	13.5

51

14 Vocabulary

14.1 TRAVEL

late

on time

pack your bags

luggage

arrive at the airport

terminal

check-in

boarding card

flight

hand luggage

security

delay

board a plane

fly in a plane

land at the airport

passport control

miss a flight

runway

set off on a journey

road trip

visit a museum

go sightseeing

get on a bus

get off a bus

hotel

apartment

hostel

cruise

arrive at a hotel

reception

stay in a hotel

leave a hotel

15 Making comparisons

A comparative adjective is used to describe the difference between two nouns. Use it before the word "than" to compare people, places, or things.

⚙ **New language** Comparative adjectives
Aa Vocabulary Travel and countries
🧩 **New skill** Comparing things

15.1 KEY LANGUAGE COMPARATIVE ADJECTIVES

For most adjectives with one or two syllables, add "er" to make the comparative.

Greece is warm.

Greece is warmer than France.

Add "er" to make the comparative.

Use "than" after the comparative adjective.

🔊

15.2 FURTHER EXAMPLES COMPARATIVE ADJECTIVES

 Ahmed is taller than **Jonathan.**

 A plane is faster than **a train.**

 5°F is colder than **85°F.**

 Sanjay is younger than **Tina.**

15.3 KEY LANGUAGE FORMING COMPARATIVES

There are special rules for adjectives ending in "e," "y," and with a single consonant.

 fast

faster

Add "er" to most adjectives of one or two syllables.

 close

closer

If the adjective ends in "e," just add "r."

 early

 earlier

For some adjectives ending in "y," take off the "y" and add "ier."

 big

 bigger

For single-syllable adjectives ending consonant-vowel-consonant, double the final letter and add "er."

15.4 FILL IN THE GAPS USING THE WORDS IN THE PANEL TO COMPLETE THE SENTENCES

The _____red_____ suitcase is bigger than the _____blue_____ suitcase.

1. An _____ is larger than a _____ .

2. _____ o'clock is earlier than _____ o'clock.

3. _____ is colder than _____ .

4. A _____ is smaller than a _____ .

red   seven   coffee   mouse   blue   three   cat   elephant   ice cream   lion

15.5 FIND NINE COMPARATIVES IN THE GRID AND WRITE THEM NEXT TO THE CORRECT ADJECTIVE

```
E R P W T I E V E H C L
H V K K R K N I A I F O
O H M E A S I E R G V W
T L A T E R C Y L H F E
T Y T X E L I C I E Q R
E F L A R G E R E R L T
R K T H I N N E R E V K
J A K I O H M R N P L Q
G D H B C L O S E R E D
```

thin = _____thinner_____

1. low = _____
2. high = _____
3. large = _____
4. late = _____
5. easy = _____
6. early = _____
7. hot = _____
8. close = _____

15.6 KEY LANGUAGE COMPARATIVES WITH LONG ADJECTIVES

For some two-syllable adjectives and those of three syllables or more, use "more" and "than" to make the comparative.

This beach is beautiful.

The adjective "beautiful" has three syllables, so you say "more beautiful than."

This beach is more beautiful than that one.

Use "more" before the adjective.

Use "than" after the adjective.

15.7 HOW TO FORM COMPARATIVES WITH LONG ADJECTIVES

SUBJECT + VERB	"MORE"	ADJECTIVE	"THAN"	REST OF SENTENCE
This beach is	more	beautiful	than	that one.

15.8 FURTHER EXAMPLES COMPARATIVES WITH LONG ADJECTIVES

 Surfing is more exciting than **going to the gym.**

 This book is more interesting than **that one.**

 Flying is more expensive than **traveling by car.**

 For me, science is more difficult than **history.**

15.9 FILL IN THE GAPS USING THE CORRECT COMPARATIVES

This movie is really exciting. It's _____*more exciting than*_____ the book.

1 The Hotel Supreme is very expensive. It's _____ the Motel Excelsior.

2 The physics exam is really difficult. It's _____ the biology exam.

3 Your dress is very beautiful. It's _____ my dress.

4 This TV program is really interesting. It's _____ the other ones.

15.10 FILL IN THE GAPS BY PUTTING THE ADJECTIVES INTO THEIR COMPARATIVE FORMS

The balloon is _____lighter than_____ (light) the birthday cake.

❶ This laptop is _____ (expensive) this phone.

❷ Seven o'clock is _____ (late) three o'clock.

❸ A game of chess is _____ (difficult) a game of cards.

❹ A horse is _____ (big) a rabbit.

🔊

15.11 LISTEN TO THE AUDIO AND ANSWER THE QUESTIONS

Selma and Joe are deciding where to go on vacation.

Costa Rica is hotter than the Bahamas.
True ✓ **False** ☐

❶ The Bahamas is easier to fly to than Costa Rica.
True ☐ **False** ☐

❷ The Bahamas is more expensive than Costa Rica.
True ☐ **False** ☐

❸ Tahiti Beach is more beautiful than Playa Hermosa.
True ☐ **False** ☐

❹ Joe thinks the Bahamas is more exciting than Costa Rica.
True ☐ **False** ☐

15.12 CROSS OUT THE INCORRECT WORDS IN EACH SENTENCE

An elephant is bigger / ~~more big~~ than a lion.

❶ Paris is beautiful / more beautiful than Dallas.

❷ Noon is earlier / more early than 5pm.

❸ A cheetah is faster / more fast than a bear.

❹ Gold is expensive / more expensive than silver.

❺ Rock is harder / more hard than paper.

❻ Water is warmer / more warm than ice.

❼ Skiing is exciting / more exciting than walking.

🔊

16 Talking about extremes

Use superlative adjectives to talk about extremes, such as "the biggest" or "the smallest." For long adjectives, use "the most" to make the superlative.

⚙ **New language** Superlative adjectives
Aa Vocabulary Animals, facts, and places
🧩 **New skill** Talking about extremes

16.1 KEY LANGUAGE SUPERLATIVE ADJECTIVES

For most adjectives with one or two syllables, add "est" to make the superlative.

The comparative describes the difference between two things.

K2 is higher than Annapurna, but Everest is the highest mountain in the world.

Always use the definite article ("the") before the superlative.

The superlative describes which thing is the most extreme.

Annapurna   K2   Everest

16.2 FURTHER EXAMPLES SUPERLATIVE ADJECTIVES

Rhinos are bigger than cows, but elephants are the biggest land animals.

Great white sharks are larger than dolphins, but blue whales are the largest animals in the world.

16.3 HOW TO FORM SENTENCES WITH SUPERLATIVES

SUBJECT + VERB	"THE" + SUPERLATIVE	REST OF SENTENCE
Everest is	the highest	**mountain in the world.**

16.4 KEY LANGUAGE FORMING SUPERLATIVES

There are special rules for adjectives ending in "e" or "y," and for some that end with a single consonant.

fast → **fastest**
Add "est" to most adjectives of one or two syllables.

close → **closest**
If the adjective ends in "e," you just add "st."

early → **earliest**
For some adjectives ending in "y," take off the "y" and add "iest."

big → **biggest**
For single-syllable adjectives ending consonant-vowel-consonant, double the final letter and add "est."

16.5 LISTEN TO THE AUDIO AND ANSWER THE QUESTIONS

Friends Joel, Sarah, and Ben talk about the things they've bought.

Who has the fastest car?
Joel ☑ Sarah ☐ Ben ☐

❶ Who is the tallest?
Joel ☐ Sarah ☐ Ben ☐

❷ Who has the smallest phone?
Joel ☐ Sarah ☐ Ben ☐

❸ Who has the cheapest laptop?
Joel ☐ Sarah ☐ Ben ☐

❹ Who has the most expensive apartment?
Joel ☐ Sarah ☐ Ben ☐

❺ Who is the youngest?
Joel ☐ Sarah ☐ Ben ☐

16.6 FILL IN THE GAPS BY PUTTING THE ADJECTIVES IN THE CORRECT FORM

The _____*oldest*_____ (old) plane in the world is the Blériot XI.

❶ The African elephant is the _____ (heavy) animal on land.

❷ The _____ (fast) animal in the world is the peregrine falcon.

❸ The _____ (long) word in the English dictionary has 45 letters.

❹ The Sahara is the _____ (big) desert in the world.

❺ The giraffe is the _____ (tall) animal on Earth.

16.7 KEY LANGUAGE SUPERLATIVES WITH LONG ADJECTIVES

For some two-syllable adjectives and for adjectives of three syllables or more, use "the most" before the adjective. The form of the adjective doesn't change.

The Palace Hotel is more expensive than the Rialto, but the Biaritz is the most expensive hotel in the city.

Use "the most" with the adjective. ⟋

The adjective stays the same.

16.8 HOW TO FORM SUPERLATIVES WITH LONG ADJECTIVES

SUBJECT + VERB	"THE" + SUPERLATIVE	ADJECTIVE	REST OF SENTENCE
This is	the most	expensive	hotel in the city.

16.9 FURTHER EXAMPLES SUPERLATIVES WITH LONG ADJECTIVES

The science museum is the most interesting museum in town.

The Twister is the most exciting ride in the theme park.

This is the most comfortable chair in the room.

16.10 MATCH THE BEGINNINGS OF THE SENTENCES TO THE CORRECT ENDINGS

The Yangtze River is	the largest state in the US.
① Antarctica is	the coldest place on Earth.
② Mumbai is	the most dangerous snake in the world.
③ Alaska is	the longest river in Asia.
④ The inland taipan is	the biggest city in India.

16.11 READ THE ARTICLE AND ANSWER THE QUESTIONS

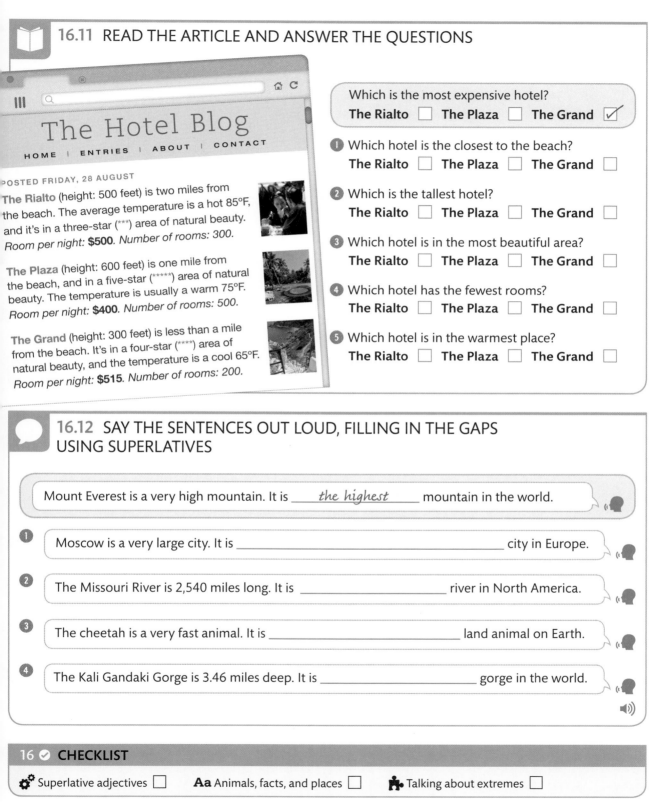

The Hotel Blog

HOME | ENTRIES | ABOUT | CONTACT

POSTED FRIDAY, 28 AUGUST

The Rialto (height: 500 feet) is two miles from the beach. The average temperature is a hot 85°F, and it's in a three-star (***) area of natural beauty. *Room per night:* **$500**. *Number of rooms: 300.*

The Plaza (height: 600 feet) is one mile from the beach, and in a five-star (*****) area of natural beauty. The temperature is usually a warm 75°F. *Room per night:* **$400**. *Number of rooms: 500.*

The Grand (height: 300 feet) is less than a mile from the beach. It's in a four-star (****) area of natural beauty, and the temperature is a cool 65°F. *Room per night:* **$515**. *Number of rooms: 200.*

Which is the most expensive hotel?
The Rialto ☐ **The Plaza** ☐ **The Grand** ☑

① Which hotel is the closest to the beach?
The Rialto ☐ **The Plaza** ☐ **The Grand** ☐

② Which is the tallest hotel?
The Rialto ☐ **The Plaza** ☐ **The Grand** ☐

③ Which hotel is in the most beautiful area?
The Rialto ☐ **The Plaza** ☐ **The Grand** ☐

④ Which hotel has the fewest rooms?
The Rialto ☐ **The Plaza** ☐ **The Grand** ☐

⑤ Which hotel is in the warmest place?
The Rialto ☐ **The Plaza** ☐ **The Grand** ☐

16.12 SAY THE SENTENCES OUT LOUD, FILLING IN THE GAPS USING SUPERLATIVES

Mount Everest is a very high mountain. It is ____*the highest*____ mountain in the world.

① Moscow is a very large city. It is _____ city in Europe.

② The Missouri River is 2,540 miles long. It is _____ river in North America.

③ The cheetah is a very fast animal. It is _____ land animal on Earth.

④ The Kali Gandaki Gorge is 3.46 miles deep. It is _____ gorge in the world.

16 ✓ CHECKLIST

⚙ Superlative adjectives ☐   **Aa** Animals, facts, and places ☐   👥 Talking about extremes ☐

17.1 GEOGRAPHICAL FEATURES

ocean

sea

coast

beach

island

cliff

rocks

cave

waterfall

countryside

field

hill

mountain

valley

canyon

sand dune

stream river pond lake

woods jungle rainforest swamp

desert oasis volcano

polar region glacier iceberg

18 Making choices

"Which," "what," "and," and "or" are all useful words to add to questions. You can use them to show whether a question is general or about specific options.

⚙ **New language** "Which" and "what"
Aa Vocabulary Geographical words
🧩 **New skill** Asking multiple-choice questions

18.1 KEY LANGUAGE "AND / OR"

Use "and" to ask about more than one thing, and "or" for choices and alternatives.

Use "or" if there is a choice.

Do you want to go to Germany or France?

France.

Do you want to go to Paris and Versailles?

Use "and" to join two things in one question.

Yes.

18.2 FURTHER EXAMPLES "AND / OR"

+ **Would you like tea and cake?**

/ **Would you like tea or coffee?**

+ **Do you have a dog and a cat?**

/ **Do you want to play golf or tennis?**

18.3 CROSS OUT THE INCORRECT WORD IN EACH SENTENCE

/ Is Mary a farmer ~~and~~ / or a teacher?

1 + Do you want to visit New York and / or Chicago?

2 / Would you like to study chemistry and / or physics?

3 + Would you like a burger and / or a soda?

4 / Do you want to go home and / or go to a restaurant?

18.4 KEY LANGUAGE "WHICH / WHAT"

You use "which" when there are two or more possibilities in the question. Use "what" when the question is more general.

There are no choices in the question.

What is the tallest building in the world?

The question includes a choice of possible answers.

Which building is taller, Big Ben or the Eiffel Tower?

18.5 FURTHER EXAMPLES "WHICH / WHAT"

What is the highest mountain in the Himalayas?

What is the fastest animal in the world?

Which mountain is higher, the Matterhorn or Mont Blanc?

Which animal is the fastest, a lion, a rhino, or a cheetah?

18.6 FILL IN THE GAPS USING "WHICH" OR "WHAT"

Which country would you like to visit, India, China, or Thailand?

❶ _____ is the biggest country in Africa?

❷ _____ would you like to eat for your dinner?

❸ _____ jacket do you want to wear, the blue one or the red one?

❹ _____ is your favorite color, red, green, yellow, or blue?

18.7 KEY LANGUAGE IRREGULAR COMPARATIVES AND SUPERLATIVES

Some common adjectives have irregular comparatives and superlatives.

ADJECTIVE	COMPARATIVE	SUPERLATIVE
good	better	best
bad	worse	worst
far	farther (US) / further (UK)	farthest (US) / furthest (UK)

TIP
In US English, "further" and "furthest" are used to describe figurative (not physical) distances.

18.8 FURTHER EXAMPLES IRREGULAR COMPARATIVES AND SUPERLATIVES

The tree is far away.

The house is farther away than the tree.

The mountain is the farthest away.

John got a good grade on his exam.

Jill got a better grade than John.

Aziz got the best grade.

New York has bad weather today.

Paris has worse weather.

London has the worst weather.

18.9 READ THE ARTICLE AND ANSWER THE QUESTIONS

Which restaurant has the best service?

The Little Olive has the best service.

1 Which has the best music?

_____

2 Which is the farthest from the beach?

_____

3 Which has the best ice cream?

_____

4 Which has the worst food?

_____

5 Which has the best seafood?

_____

GREAT FOOD MAGAZINE

PLACES TO EAT
Where to go for dinner this weekend

THE LITTLE OLIVE – This restaurant is five minutes from the beach. It has no live music, but the food is great and its seafood is the best in town. The service here is excellent.

JOHN'S BAR – This is a great place to listen to music. It's on the beach and has bands every night. The food and service are OK.

SEAVIEW CAFÉ – This café is two minutes from the beach. It doesn't have music, but the food and service aren't bad. Go here for the ice cream, it's the best in town.

THE BIG CAHUNA – They play OK music here, but the food and service are not good. It's more than ten minutes from the beach, but it has the best views in town.

18.10 LISTEN TO THE AUDIO AND ANSWER THE QUESTIONS

Rita Adams answers questions on a TV game show.

Which is the largest US state?
Texas ☐ **Virginia** ☐ **Alaska** ☑

1 Which city is farthest from the equator?
Taipei ☐ **Bangkok** ☐ **Manila** ☐

2 Which is the smallest South American country?
Brazil ☐ **Peru** ☐ **Suriname** ☐

3 Which is the biggest desert?
Mojave ☐ **Sahara** ☐ **Kalahari** ☐

4 Which is the tallest building?
Big Ben ☐ **Eiffel Tower** ☐ **Pisa Tower** ☐

5 Which is the highest mountain?
K2 ☐ **Kilimanjaro** ☐ **Mont Blanc** ☐

18 ✓ CHECKLIST

⚙ "Which" and "what" ☐   **Aa** Geographical words ☐   Asking multiple-choice questions ☐

19 Using large numbers

You usually write numbers larger than 100 in figures. To say them, add "and" in front of the number signified by the last two digits, such as "one hundred and ten."

⚙ **New language** Large numbers
Aa Vocabulary Thousands and millions
🧩 **New skill** Talking about large amounts

19.1 KEY LANGUAGE LARGE NUMBERS

You can say "one hundred" or "a hundred." Both are correct. Don't add "s" to "hundred," "thousand," or "million."

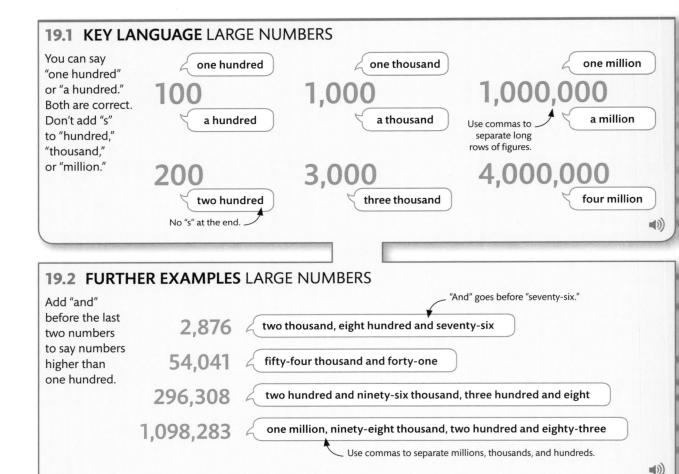

one hundred
100
a hundred

one thousand
1,000
a thousand

one million
1,000,000
a million

Use commas to separate long rows of figures.

200
two hundred
No "s" at the end.

3,000
three thousand

4,000,000
four million

19.2 FURTHER EXAMPLES LARGE NUMBERS

Add "and" before the last two numbers to say numbers higher than one hundred.

"And" goes before "seventy-six."

2,876 — two thousand, eight hundred and seventy-six

54,041 — fifty-four thousand and forty-one

296,308 — two hundred and ninety-six thousand, three hundred and eight

1,098,283 — one million, ninety-eight thousand, two hundred and eighty-three

Use commas to separate millions, thousands, and hundreds.

19.3 LISTEN TO THE AUDIO AND MARK THE NUMBERS YOU HEAR

513 ☐
530 ☑

❶ 4,500 ☐
   40,500 ☐

❷ 476,000 ☐
   467,000 ☐

❸ 989 ☐
   999 ☐

❹ 72,427 ☐
   72,247 ☐

❺ 4,125,125 ☐
   4,125,025 ☐

19.4 SAY THE NUMBERS OUT LOUD

532	*five hundred and thirty-two*

❶ 3,107

❷ 23,417

❸ 345,972

❹ 23,456,987

---

19 ✓ CHECKLIST

⚙ Large numbers ☐   **Aa** Thousands and millions ☐   Talking about large amounts ☐

↻ REVIEW THE ENGLISH YOU HAVE LEARNED IN UNITS 15-19

NEW LANGUAGE	SAMPLE SENTENCE	☑	UNIT
COMPARATIVE ADJECTIVES	Greece is warmer than France.	☐	15.1, 15.3, 15.6
SUPERLATIVE ADJECTIVES	K2 is higher than Annapurna, but Everest is the highest mountain in the world.	☐	16.1, 16.4, 16.7
"AND" AND "OR"	Do you want to go to Germany or France? Do you want to go to Paris and Versailles?	☐	18.1, 18.2
"WHICH" AND "WHAT"	What is the tallest building? Which mountain is higher, the Matterhorn or Mont Blanc?	☐	18.4, 18.5
LARGE NUMBERS	Two thousand, eight hundred and seventy-six	☐	19.1, 19.2

20 Vocabulary

20.1 THE CALENDAR

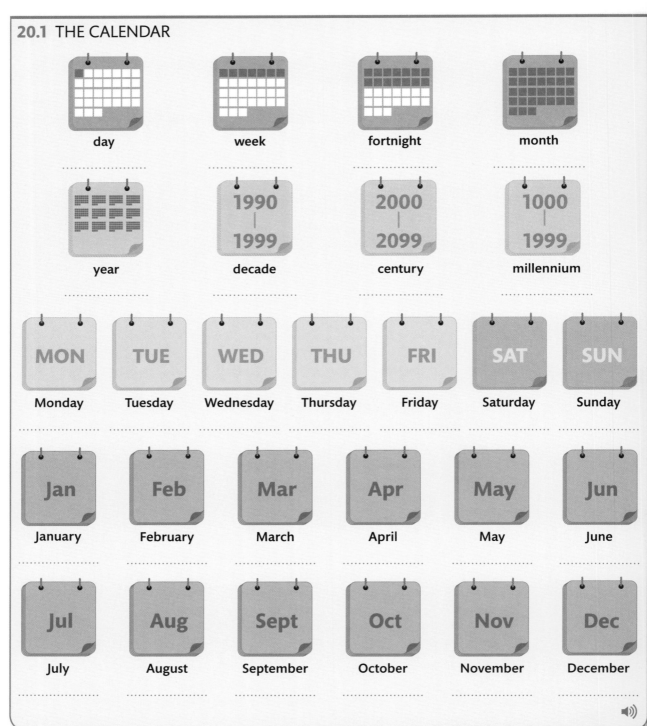

day

week

fortnight

month

year

decade

century

millennium

MON — Monday

TUE — Tuesday

WED — Wednesday

THU — Thursday

FRI — Friday

SAT — Saturday

SUN — Sunday

Jan — January

Feb — February

Mar — March

Apr — April

May — May

Jun — June

Jul — July

Aug — August

Sept — September

Oct — October

Nov — November

Dec — December

20.2 SEASONS

spring

summer

fall (US)
autumn (UK)

winter

20.3 ORDINAL NUMBERS

1st first	**2nd** second	**3rd** third	**4th** fourth
5th fifth	**6th** sixth	**7th** seventh	**8th** eighth
9th ninth	**10th** tenth	**11th** eleventh	**12th** twelfth
13th thirteenth	**14th** fourteenth	**15th** fifteenth	**16th** sixteenth
17th seventeenth	**18th** eighteenth	**19th** nineteenth	**20th** twentieth
21st twenty-first	**22nd** twenty-second	**23rd** twenty-third	**24th** twenty-fourth
25th twenty-fifth	**26th** twenty-sixth	**27th** twenty-seventh	**28th** twenty-eighth
29th twenty-ninth	**30th** thirtieth	**31st** thirty-first	

21 Talking about dates

There are two different ways of writing and saying dates. You use numbers along with the month to define the date you're talking about.

⚙ **New language** Dates, "was born," "ago"
Aa Vocabulary Numbers, months, and years
🧩 **New skill** Talking about dates

21.1 KEY LANGUAGE WRITING AND SAYING DATES

In the US, people often describe dates by writing cardinal numbers and saying ordinal numbers.

The number comes after the month.

His meeting is on May 10.
> May tenth

My birthday is on May 18.
> May eighteenth

The party is on May 31.
> May thirty-first

🔊

21.2 ANOTHER WAY TO SAY IT WRITING AND SAYING DATES

In some other places, such as the UK, people use ordinal numbers to write and say dates.

His meeting is on the 10th of May.
> the tenth of May

My birthday is on May the 18th.
> May the eighteenth

The party is on the 31st of May.
> the thirty-first of May

🔊

21.3 LISTEN TO THE AUDIO, THEN NUMBER THE DATES IN THE ORDER THEY ARE DISCUSSED

ⓐ November 17 ☐   **ⓑ** March 22 1   **ⓒ** September 13 ☐   **ⓓ** May 19 ☐

ⓔ August 31 ☐   **ⓕ** April 5 ☐   **ⓖ** June 5 ☐

21.4 KEY LANGUAGE USING "WAS BORN"

Use "was born" to talk about someone's date or year of birth.

Jim was born in { 1975. 2015.

nineteen seventy-five

You say most dates by grouping the date into pairs of numbers, such as "nineteen" and "seventy-five."

twenty fifteen

You can say "two thousand and fifteen" or "twenty fifteen."

◀))

21.5 KEY LANGUAGE USING "AGO"

You use "ago" to say how many years before now something happened.

Plato was born around 2,500 years ago, in 424 BCE.

"Ago" means "before now."

◀))

21.6 LISTEN TO THE AUDIO AND NOTE THE YEAR OF EACH EVENT

1971

① ② ③ ④ ⑤

21.7 USE THE CHART TO CREATE 12 CORRECT SENTENCES AND SAY THEM OUT LOUD

My birthday is on December 5.

| My Nami's I He | birthday meeting | is on | December 5. the 11th of March. |
| | was born | 20 41 | years ago. |

◀))

22 Talking about the past

The past simple describes events that happened
at a definite time in the past, or the state of
things at a particular point in time.

⚙ **New language** The past simple of "to be"
Aa Vocabulary Jobs, town, and life events
🧩 **New skill** Talking about past states

22.1 KEY LANGUAGE THE PAST SIMPLE OF "TO BE"

Any action that
happened and was
completed in the
past can be
described in the past
simple. The past
simple of "to be"
is "was" or "were."

This is the present simple.

Jill is a businesswoman now.
She was a student in 1985.

This is the
past simple.

This is a definite
time in the past.

22.2 HOW TO FORM THE PAST SIMPLE OF "TO BE"

The past simple
of "to be" changes
with the subject.

SUBJECT	"TO BE"	REST OF SENTENCE
I	was	
You	were	a student.
He / She / It	was	
We / They / You	were	students.

22.3 FURTHER EXAMPLES THE PAST SIMPLE OF "TO BE"

He was **a doctor for 40 years.**

She was **a Broadway star in the 1960s.**

There was **a party last night.**

We were **at the library yesterday.**

There were **lots of people at the party.**

They were **at the movies last week.**

22.4 CROSS OUT THE INCORRECT WORD IN EACH SENTENCE

She **was** / ~~were~~ a teacher.

1 You **was** / **were** at the museum last week.

2 There **was** / **were** five people here yesterday.

3 The students **was** / **were** there on Monday morning.

4 My mom **was** / **were** an artist in the 1990s.

5 I **was** / **were** in college in 1989.

6 Sal and I **was** / **were** at the theater last night.

7 My dad **was** / **were** a builder until 1995.

🔊

22.5 READ THE EMAIL AND ANSWER THE QUESTIONS

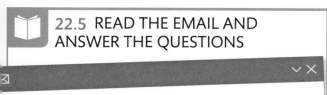

To: Jules

Subject: Weekend in L.A.

How are you? I was in Los Angeles on the weekend. I was at Manhattan Beach. Do you know it? It was very hot and there were lots of people there. There are many cafés there, too. I was in a café called Ocean View and Malcolm was there. He was with a woman called Stacey. Is she his girlfriend?....

Annie x

Annie was in Los Angeles on the weekend.
True ✓ **False** ☐

1 She was at Manhattan Beach.
True ☐ **False** ☐

2 It was cold there.
True ☐ **False** ☐

3 She was at a café called Sea View.
True ☐ **False** ☐

4 Her friend Malcolm was with another man.
True ☐ **False** ☐

22.6 LISTEN TO THE AUDIO AND MATCH THE EVENTS TO THE YEARS

Chat Radio give the answers to their "That Was The Day" quiz.

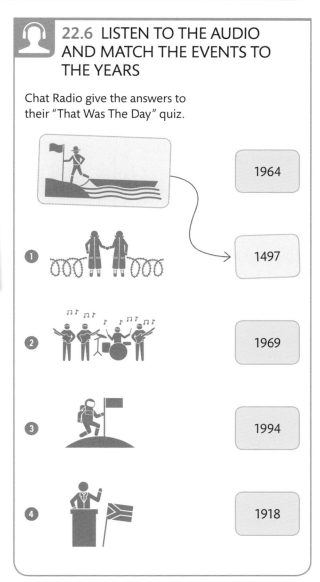

22.7 KEY LANGUAGE "WAS" / "WERE" NEGATIVES

As in the present simple, use "not" to form negative statements in the past simple.

Add "not" after "was" or "were."

He { was not / wasn't } a teacher in 2004.

They { were not / weren't } at the park yesterday.

You can contract these negatives to their short forms.

22.8 KEY LANGUAGE "WAS" / "WERE" QUESTIONS

To ask questions about the past using the verb "to be," swap the subject and verb.

He was in India.

Was he in India?

Swap the subject and "to be."

They were late for school.

Were they late for school?

22.9 FURTHER EXAMPLES "WAS" / "WERE" NEGATIVES AND QUESTIONS

I wasn't a good waiter.

Were there any cakes at the party?

There weren't any boats.

Was he good at playing tennis?

22.10 CROSS OUT THE INCORRECT WORD IN EACH SENTENCE

He wasn't / ~~weren't~~ a doctor.

1 They wasn't / weren't very good at science.

2 I wasn't / weren't in Canada in 2002.

3 You wasn't / weren't at the party last night.

4 We wasn't / weren't in our house last year.

5 There wasn't / weren't a restaurant near the river.

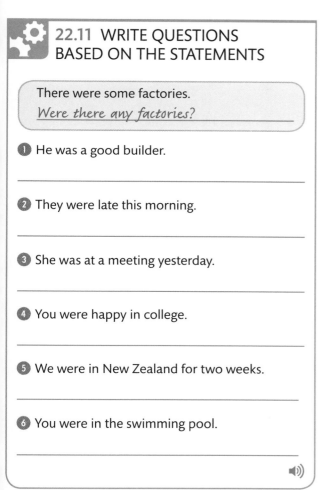

22.11 WRITE QUESTIONS BASED ON THE STATEMENTS

There were some factories.
Were there any factories?

1 He was a good builder.

2 They were late this morning.

3 She was at a meeting yesterday.

4 You were happy in college.

5 We were in New Zealand for two weeks.

6 You were in the swimming pool.

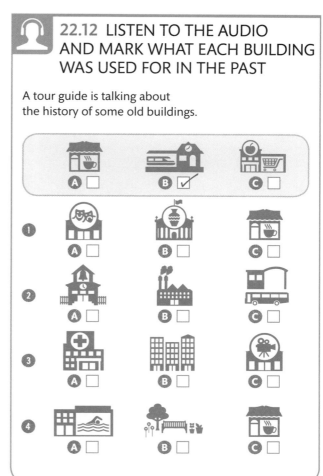

22.12 LISTEN TO THE AUDIO AND MARK WHAT EACH BUILDING WAS USED FOR IN THE PAST

A tour guide is talking about the history of some old buildings.

22.13 USE THE CHART TO CREATE 15 CORRECT SENTENCES AND SAY THEM OUT LOUD

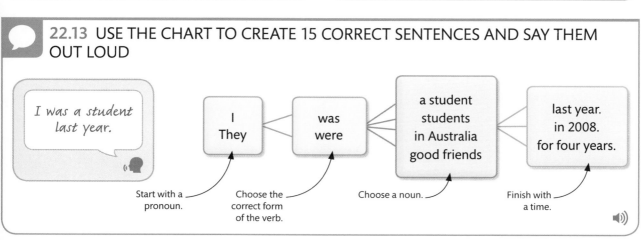

I was a student last year.

| I / They | was / were | a student / students / in Australia / good friends | last year. / in 2008. / for four years. |

Start with a pronoun. — Choose the correct form of the verb. — Choose a noun. — Finish with a time.

23 Past events

Some verbs are regular in the past simple. You can use a lot of them to talk about the past week, the last year, or your life. Their past simple forms ends in "-ed."

⚙ **New language** Regular verbs in the past simple
Aa **Vocabulary** Pastimes and life events
🧩 **New skill** Talking about your past

23.1 KEY LANGUAGE REGULAR VERBS IN THE PAST SIMPLE

The past simple describes events that happened in the past. The past simple forms of regular verbs end in "-ed." The negative uses "did not" plus the base form.

The verb ends in "-ed."

I **visited** Luke last Friday.

He didn't play **tennis last night.**

23.2 HOW TO FORM REGULAR VERBS IN THE PAST SIMPLE

The past forms of most verbs do not change with the subject. Use the past simple of "do" plus the base verb to form negative statements.

Use the same form for all subjects.

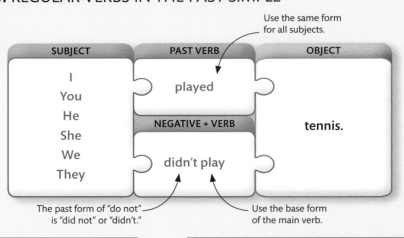

SUBJECT	PAST VERB	OBJECT
I You He She We They	played	tennis.
	NEGATIVE + VERB	
	didn't play	

The past form of "do not" is "did not" or "didn't."

Use the base form of the main verb.

23.3 FURTHER EXAMPLES REGULAR VERBS IN THE PAST SIMPLE

Questions are formed using "did" + subject + the base form of the verb.

He walked **to the office.**

Did they work **late?**

She didn't walk **downtown.**

We didn't watch **TV today.**

23.4 FILL IN THE GAPS BY PUTTING THE VERBS IN THE PAST SIMPLE

Last Friday, I _____ *cooked* _____ (cook 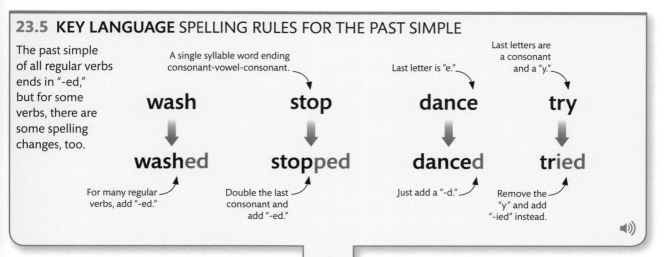) a meal for my friends.

❶ The music was good, but I _____ (not dance) very much.

❷ My friend _____ (not listen) to the band on Saturday night.

❸ Last week, I _____ (clean) my brother's new car for him.

❹ Did you _____ (watch) a fun movie last night?

❺ Ben and Franklin _____ (play) tennis for five hours yesterday.

23.5 KEY LANGUAGE SPELLING RULES FOR THE PAST SIMPLE

The past simple of all regular verbs ends in "-ed," but for some verbs, there are some spelling changes, too.

A single syllable word ending consonant-vowel-consonant.

Last letter is "e."

Last letters are a consonant and a "y."

wash → **washed**
For many regular verbs, add "-ed."

stop → **stopped**
Double the last consonant and add "-ed."

dance → **danced**
Just add a "-d."

try → **tried**
Remove the "y" and add "-ied" instead.

23.6 FURTHER EXAMPLES SPELLING RULES FOR THE PAST SIMPLE

He carried **the bags for her.**

We arrived **here at midnight.**

I studied **English last year.**

They saved **money for a vacation.**

23.7 LOOK AT JOYCE'S DIARY FROM LAST WEEK AND FILL IN THE GAPS TO COMPLETE THE SENTENCES

WEEKLY PLANNER

MONDAY
Evening: watch movie on TV

TUESDAY
Morning: play squash
Afternoon: phone my boss

WEDNESDAY
try sushi at Japanese restaurant

THURSDAY
Morning: clean the bathroom
Night: visit Aziz in hospital

FRIDAY
invite friends to my birthday party

SATURDAY
walk in the park

SUNDAY
cook dinner for my parents

On Monday evening, Joyce ___*watched*___ a movie on TV.

① On Tuesday morning, she _____ squash.

② On Tuesday afternoon, she _____ her boss.

③ On Wednesday, she _____ sushi at a Japanese restaurant.

④ On Thursday morning, she _____ the bathroom.

⑤ On Thursday night, she _____ Aziz in hospital.

⑥ On Friday, she _____ friends to her birthday party.

⑦ On Saturday, she _____ in the park.

⑧ On Sunday, she _____ dinner for her parents.

◀))

 23.8 LISTEN TO THE AUDIO AND MATCH THE EVENTS TO THE YEARS

Arno describes his life so far.
He mentions important events and
the years in which they happened.

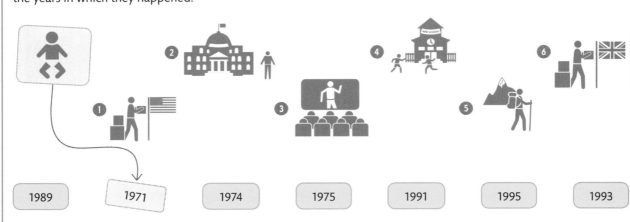

23.9 KEY LANGUAGE USING "WHEN" WITH THE PAST SIMPLE

To say when in someone's life something happened, you can either use "in" with the year, or "when" with the person's age.

This is the past simple action.

He moved to England in 1990.

He moved to England when he was 10 years old.

This describes when in the past it happened.

23.10 REWRITE THE SENTENCES ADDING "WHEN" CLAUSES

I started school (four years old). = *I started school when I was four years old.*

1. She moved to the US (19 years old). = _____

2. They started swimming (25 years old). = _____

3. We visited Japan (27 years old). = _____

4. I received this gift (31 years old). = _____

23.11 LOOK AT LEONA'S LIFE EVENTS, THEN DESCRIBE EACH ONE OUT LOUD

BORN	MOVE TO NEW YORK	VISIT ASIA	START FIRST JOB
1988	1996	2008	2010

She was born in 1988.

1.

2.

3.

---

24 Past abilities

In the past simple, "can" becomes "could."
You often use it to talk about things you
"could" do in the past, but can't do now.

New language Using "could" in the past simple

Aa Vocabulary Abilities and pastimes

New skill Talking about past abilities

24.1 KEY LANGUAGE "COULD" FOR PAST ABILITIES

Use "could" to talk about an ability you once had. You can
use "when" plus a time setting to say when you had the ability.

Set the time frame with a phrase
about an age, day, or year.

 I can't **climb trees now, but** I could **when I was younger.**

You can use the present
simple for contrast.

The statement can be positive using "could" or
negative using "couldn't." It doesn't change with
the subject.

24.2 FURTHER EXAMPLES "COULD" FOR PAST ABILITIES

When I was a student, I could **study all night before an exam.**

I couldn't **go to China last year because it was too expensive.**

When Milo was eight, he could **play the violin.**

Last year, she couldn't **run very far, but yesterday she ran a marathon.**

24.3 HOW TO FORM "COULD" FOR PAST ABILITIES

"WHEN"	TIME SETTING	"COULD"	ABILITY
When	**I was younger,**	**I could** **I couldn't**	**climb trees.**

Begin with
"when."

This phrase sets the
time in the past when
the action was possible.

The statement can be
positive or negative.

Use the base form of the
verb for the past ability.

24.4 REWRITE THESE SENTENCES IN THE PAST SIMPLE USING "COULD"

I can ski.	I could ski.
① I can cook Italian food.	
② We can't play the piano.	
③ She can paint a picture.	
④ They can't make a cake.	

24.5 LISTEN TO THE AUDIO AND MARK THE CORRECT ANSWERS

When Diana was five, she couldn't...
write music ✓
read music ☐
play the piano. ☐

② When Imelda was seven, she could...
ride a horse ☐
drive a car ☐
fly a plane. ☐

① When Louis was four, he could...
read ☐
write ☐
do mathematics. ☐

③ When Irina was four, she could speak...
one language ☐
two languages ☐
three languages. ☐

24.6 USE THE CHART TO CREATE 16 CORRECT SENTENCES AND SAY THEM OUT LOUD

When I was five, I couldn't play chess.

When I was / When you were → five, seven, → I couldn't / you could → play chess. ride a bike. swim. skate.

Start with a "when" phrase.

Choose an age.

Choose a positive or negative statement.

Finish with an ability.

25 Vocabulary

25.1 ENTERTAINMENT

movie (US)
film (UK)

novel

play

TV show

the news

newspaper

magazine

comedy

science fiction

thriller

documentary

action

horror

musical

romance

crime

hero

villain

audience

clap

movie star (US)
film star (UK)

actor

main character

director

author

plot

special effects

stunt

movie theater (US)
cinema (UK)

theater (US)
theatre (UK)

bookstore (US)
bookshop (UK)

exhibition

26 Irregular past verbs

In the past simple, some verbs are irregular. Their past simple forms are not formed using the normal rules, and sometimes look very different from the infinitive forms.

⚙ **New language** Irregular verbs in the past simple
Aa Vocabulary Sequence words
🧩 **New skill** Describing the past

26.1 KEY LANGUAGE IRREGULAR VERBS IN THE PAST SIMPLE

"Go" is the present simple.

I often go to the movies.

I went last night, but I didn't go last week.

"Went" is the past simple of "go."

To make the negative, use "didn't" with the base form.

26.2 HOW TO FORM IRREGULAR VERBS IN THE PAST SIMPLE

Verbs in the past simple do not change with the subject.

This is the past simple of "go."

| SUBJECT | VERB | |
| I | went | to the movies. |

| SUBJECT | NEGATIVE | VERB | |
| I | didn't | go | to the movies. |

Use "did not" or "didn't" to make the negative.

Use the base form of the main verb in the negative.

26.3 FURTHER EXAMPLES IRREGULAR VERBS IN THE PAST SIMPLE

They had **a great vacation.** He didn't have **any classes today.**

I came **to the US in 1980.** You didn't come **to the party.**

Aa 26.4 MATCH THE PAST SIMPLE FORMS OF THE VERBS TO THEIR BASE FORMS

put	break	⑤ bought	get
① began	put	⑥ got	buy
② broke	take	⑦ wrote	make
③ took	sell	⑧ made	sit
④ sold	begin	⑨ sat	write

26.5 READ THE ARTICLE AND NUMBER THE PICTURES IN THE ORDER THEY ARE DESCRIBED

WILD ADVENTURES

A lucky escape!

A VERY WILD ADVENTURE IN THE FOREST

A few years ago I went camping in Redwood Park with my best friend, Jack. On our first day, we bought some food. We didn't want to stay on the campsite, so instead we walked through the forest to find somewhere else to camp. It got dark early and we were a bit lost so we decided to camp in the middle of the forest. That night, it was really dark and I felt a bit scared, but Jack and I made a fire and sang some songs. It was a quiet night and we slept well.

In the morning, we were hungry so we made our breakfast. But before we ate it, we went to the river.

We had a wash and got some fresh water then walked back to our tent. When we got back to the tent, we saw a big brown bear. We didn't move or make a noise. We watched the bear as it sat in our tent and ate all of our breakfast. After that it walked off into the forest with our bags.

Jack and I were very hungry and cold, but we put our tent away and walked away quickly. Then, we ran and ran until finally we found the campsite. We were so happy. It was a very lucky escape!

 A ☐   B ☐   C ☐1   D ☐   E ☐   F ☐   G ☐

26.6 FILL IN THE GAPS IN THIS JOURNAL USING THE WORDS IN THE PANEL

Wow! This morning a bear ___ate___ my breakfast. We are in Redwood Park and last night we camped in the forest. We _____ a fire and it was very quiet, so my friend and I _____ well. The next morning, we _____ to the river to get water. When we got back to the tent, we _____ the bear. I _____ really scared. We _____ back to the campsite and we are safe now!

| ate | slept | made | went | felt | saw | ran |

26.7 VOCABULARY SEQUENCE WORDS

You use certain words and phrases to help someone understand where you are in the story.

First he
woke up.

Then he
ate breakfast.

Next he
had a shower.

After that he
got dressed.

Finally he
went to work.

26.8 FURTHER EXAMPLES SEQUENCE WORDS

First I got some money
out of the bank.

Then I bought some
food from the supermarket.

After that
I had some coffee.

In the morning we watched
the sun rise over the Serengeti.

Then we saw
the birds fly off.

Finally the
lions appeared.

26.9 REWRITE THE SENTENCES PUTTING THE SEQUENCE WORDS IN THE CORRECT PLACES

I won the game. I got a prize. (then)
I won the game. Then I got a prize.

❶ Sheila put her best clothes on. (first)

_____

❷ Do your homework. Go out and play. (first, then)

_____

❸ Ben passed his test. He bought a car. (next)

_____

❹ Eat dinner. You can have some dessert. (after that)

_____

❺ He ate a large breakfast. (first)

_____

◀))

26.10 FILL IN THE GAPS USING SEQUENCE WORDS, THEN SAY THE STORY OUT LOUD

____First____ Harold and Jack bought some food. ____Then____ they went to the forest.

❶ _____ they got lost. Then they decided to camp and put the tent up.

❷ They were scared of the sounds in the forest. But _____ they went to sleep.

❸ _____ they washed in the river. They went back to their tent for food.

❹ _____ they saw a bear eating their food. After that it walked into the forest.

❺ _____ Harold and Jack arrived safely back at the campsite.

~~first~~	after that	~~then~~	finally
finally		after that	in the morning

◀))

89

26.11 KEY LANGUAGE IRREGULAR VERBS, QUESTIONS IN THE PAST SIMPLE

Use the past simple of "do" plus
the base verb form to ask a question.

In the statement the main
verb is in the past simple.

They bought a new car.

Did they buy a new car?

"Did" is in the
past simple of "do."

The main verb
is in its base form.

She saw the show last night.

Did she see the show last night?

26.12 FURTHER EXAMPLES IRREGULAR VERBS, QUESTIONS IN THE PAST SIMPLE

Did they have **a good time?**

Did you read **a book on the beach?**

Did she meet **her friends in town?**

Did he go **to the gym?**

Aa 26.13 MATCH THE QUESTIONS AND ANSWERS

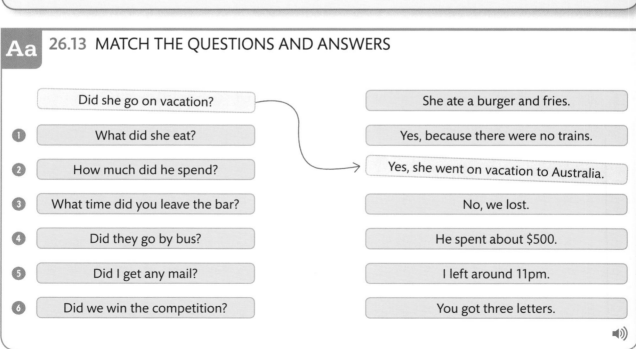

Did she go on vacation? — Yes, she went on vacation to Australia.

1. What did she eat? — She ate a burger and fries.

2. How much did he spend? — He spent about $500.

3. What time did you leave the bar? — I left around 11pm.

4. Did they go by bus? — Yes, because there were no trains.

5. Did I get any mail? — You got three letters.

6. Did we win the competition? — No, we lost.

26.14 FILL IN THE GAPS TO WRITE QUESTIONS BASED ON THE SENTENCES

They sold 50 cakes.

How many ___cakes did they sell?___

❶ The movie began at 7:30pm.

When _____

❷ He chose the red shirt.

Which_____

❸ She ate pasta last night.

What _____

❹ She read the magazine this morning.

What _____

❺ Aia caught five fish at the lake.

How many _____

❻ You saw Michelle at the party last night.

Who _____

❼ He gave his brother a new sweater.

What _____

26.15 LISTEN TO THE AUDIO AND ANSWER THE QUESTIONS

Daniella and Marcus are talking about their friend's birthday party.

When did Daniella arrive at the party?

7pm ☐
8pm ☑
9pm ☐

❶ What did she wear?

a red dress ☐
a green skirt ☐
her jeans ☐

❷ What gift did she give her friend?

a watch ☐
flowers ☐
a book ☐

❸ Who did she meet at the party?

Sam ☐
Lana ☐
Will ☐

❹ What did she eat at the party?

burger ☐
pizza ☐
chicken ☐

❺ Which music did she dance to?

jazz ☐
rock ☐
pop ☐

27 Vocabulary

27.1 TOOLS

tape measure	hammer	clamp	file	hacksaw
screwdriver	nut	bolt	screw	nail
pliers	wrench (US) spanner (UK)			
trowel	shears	fork	spade	hoe	rake

saw

drill

jigsaw

level (US)
spirit level (UK)

27.2 KITCHEN IMPLEMENTS

grater

peeler

whisk

cutting board (US)
chopping board (UK)

kitchen knife

scissors

can opener (US)
tin opener (UK)

bottle opener

corkscrew

wooden spoon

spatula

ladle

28 Telling a story

You can use "about" to describe the subject matter of movies, shows, and stories. Use adjectives to make a description more specific.

🔧 **New language** "About," opinions
Aa Vocabulary Opinions
🧩 **New skill** Describing media and culture

28.1 KEY LANGUAGE USING "ABOUT" TO DESCRIBE MEDIA AND CULTURE

Use "about" to give more information about a movie, play, show, story, or book.

It's a movie
It's a story
The play is

about

a mystery.
a lawyer.
two brothers.

This introduces what the subject matter of the story is.

This is the additional information on the story.

28.2 FURTHER EXAMPLES USING "ABOUT" TO DESCRIBE MEDIA AND CULTURE

The movie is a thriller about two New York police officers.

It's a story about a young couple in the countryside.

The book is about a French city during the 1920s.

28.3 LISTEN TO THE AUDIO AND NUMBER THE MOVIES IN THE ORDER THEY ARE DESCRIBED

28.4 KEY LANGUAGE DESCRIBING YOUR OPINIONS

You can use verbs in the past simple to give your opinions. Use "because" plus adjectives to give your reasons.

Use a positive verb... ...with a positive adjective.

I { liked / enjoyed / loved } the play because it was { funny. / romantic. / thrilling. }

Kahil { didn't enjoy / didn't like / hated } the show because it was { boring. / slow. / silly. }

Use a negative verb... ...with a negative adjective.

28.5 LISTEN TO THE AUDIO AND ANSWER THE QUESTIONS

Two friends discuss the play they've just seen.

Chrissy enjoyed the play.
True ✓ **False** ☐

❶ Jack hated it.
True ☐ **False** ☐

❷ The story was exciting.
True ☐ **False** ☐

❸ The actors were good.
True ☐ **False** ☐

❹ The villain was scary.
True ☐ **False** ☐

❺ The hero was brave.
True ☐ **False** ☐

❻ The music was great.
True ☐ **False** ☐

28.6 USE THE CHART TO CREATE 12 CORRECT SENTENCES AND SAY THEM OUT LOUD

The movie is about three characters.

| The / It's a | movie / play | is about / about | three characters. / a court case. / a love story. |

28.7 READ THE REVIEW AND ANSWER THE QUESTIONS

> What type of show is it?
> *It is a musical.*

1 What does Millie enjoy?

_____

2 Where does she learn to sing?

_____

3 What is the name of her music teacher?

_____

4 Who is the villain?

_____

5 Is Millie played by an adult?

_____

STAGE REVIEW

Millie's Magic!
The latest show in town is a hit

Millie's Magical Music is a wonderful new show. The story is about a little girl called Millie. She loves singing. In her bedroom, she listens to songs and learns how to sing them. At school, she has a kind English teacher called Miss Graham and a terrible music teacher called Miss Cafferty, who is the villain of the story. Both Miss Graham and Miss Cafferty hear Millie's beautiful voice. Miss Graham wants everyone to hear Millie, but Miss Cafferty wants to stop her singing.

It's an enjoyable story about music, friendship, and hope.

Many of the actors in this musical are children and they are all excellent, especially Millie. The songs in the musical are very good, too.

I really liked the music. It's a hit!

 28.8 REWRITE THESE SENTENCES USING NEGATIVE WORDS

> The musical was **wonderful**.
> *The musical was awful.*

1 Millie **loves** singing.

_____

2 Millie has **beautiful** costumes.

_____

3 Many of the actors were **excellent**.

_____

4 The songs are very **good**.

_____

5 I really **loved** the music.

_____

| bad | hated | ~~awful~~ | hates | terrible | ugly |

Aa 28.9 READ THE CLUES AND WRITE THE ANSWERS IN THE GRID

① The bad guy, the hero fights this person

② A true story with real people, not actors

③ A funny story that makes people laugh

④ A story told in a theater

⑤ A person who writes novels

⑥ An exciting story

adventure   author   play

comedy   ~~villain~~   documentary

¹v i l l ⁶a i n

2

3

---

28 ✔ CHECKLIST

⚙ "About," opinions ☐   **Aa** Opinions ☐   🧩 Describing media and culture ☐

↻ REVIEW THE ENGLISH YOU HAVE LEARNED IN UNITS 21–28

NEW LANGUAGE	SAMPLE SENTENCE	☑	UNIT
WRITING AND SAYING DATES	His birthday is on May 10. My meeting is on the 18th of May.	☐	21.1, 21.2
"TO BE" STATEMENTS AND QUESTIONS ABOUT THE PAST	She was a student in 1985. Was he in India last year? He wasn't in France.	☐	22.1, 22.7, 22.8
REGULAR VERBS IN THE PAST SIMPLE	I visited Luke last Friday. I didn't play tennis.	☐	23.1
USING "COULD" FOR PAST ABILITIES	I could climb trees when I was younger.	☐	24.1
IRREGULAR VERBS IN THE PAST SIMPLE	I went to the movies last night. I didn't go last week.	☐	26.1
GIVING OPINIONS ABOUT CULTURE	It's a movie about two brothers. I enjoyed it because it was thrilling.	☐	28.1, 28.4

29 Asking about the past

You can make questions in the past simple using "did." This is useful for asking about past events, such as travel and vacations.

⚙ **New language** Past simple questions
Aa Vocabulary Travel and activities
🧩 **New skill** Talking about vacations

29.1 KEY LANGUAGE "YES / NO" QUESTIONS IN THE PAST SIMPLE

Use the auxiliary verb "did" to make questions in the past simple that have "yes/no" answers.

"Did" goes before the subject.

Did you have a good holiday?

Yes, we went to India.

Did you visit the Taj Mahal?

The verb after "did" goes in its base form.

No, we didn't.

Use "did" or "didn't" for short answers.

29.2 FURTHER EXAMPLES "YES / NO" QUESTIONS IN THE PAST SIMPLE

Did you see any tigers?

Yes, I did.

Did he stay in the five-star hotel?

"Did" doesn't change with the subject.

No, he didn't.

Did they buy any ice cream?

Yes, they did.

Did we bring enough money with us?

No, we didn't.

29.3 HOW TO FORM "YES / NO" QUESTIONS IN THE PAST SIMPLE

"DID"	SUBJECT	VERB	OBJECT
Did	you	visit	the Taj Mahal?

29.4 LISTEN TO THE AUDIO, THEN NUMBER THE PICTURES IN THE ORDER THEY ARE DESCRIBED

Bea talks about her vacation in India.

A ☐

B 1

C ☐

D ☐

E ☐

29.5 MATCH THE QUESTIONS TO THE SHORT ANSWERS

Did you get the job? — Yes, we did.

❶ Did I have lunch today? → Yes, I did.

❷ Did the dog eat its dinner? — No, you didn't.

❸ Did they go to Venezuela? — Yes, it did.

❹ Did we win the competition? — No, they didn't.

🔊

29.6 REWRITE THE SENTENCES AS QUESTIONS

They went paragliding in Greece.
Did they go paragliding in Greece?

❶ They gave Ellie a present.
_____

❷ You stayed in an expensive hotel.
_____

❸ His mother bought a lot of postcards.
_____

❹ Your brother climbed a mountain.
_____

❺ Their parents took lots of photos.
_____

🔊

29.7 KEY LANGUAGE QUESTION WORDS WITH THE PAST SIMPLE

The question word goes at the beginning of the question, followed by "did" and the subject.

The question word goes at the beginning.

When did you arrive at the hotel?

Yesterday.

How did you get here?

By taxi.

The verb after "did" goes in its base form.

29.8 FURTHER EXAMPLES QUESTION WORDS WITH THE PAST SIMPLE

Where did you go on vacation?

We went to Paris.

What did you see in Paris?

The Eiffel Tower.

What did you do on vacation?

We went hiking.

When did you come home?

This morning.

29.9 MATCH THE QUESTIONS WITH THE CORRECT ANSWERS

What time did you arrive at the hotel? — At 10pm.

By taxi.

1. How did you get to the station?

Daniella and Toni.

2. Where did you stay?

Because it was cheap.

3. Why did you stay there?

At 10pm.

4. Who did you go on vacation with?

In the Hotel Bella Vista.

29.10 READ THE EMAIL AND ANSWER THE QUESTIONS

When did she arrive in New York?
On Monday ☐ **On Thursday** ☐ **On Friday** ☑

1 How did she get to Staten Island?
By taxi ☐ **By boat** ☐ **By bus** ☐

2 When did she see the Statue of Liberty?
On Friday ☐ **On Saturday** ☐ **Yesterday** ☐

3 Which store did she go to?
Macy's ☐ **Bloomingdale's** ☐ **Saks Fifth Avenue** ☐

4 What did she buy there?
Some shoes ☐ **Some perfume** ☐ **Some clothes** ☐

5 What did Sue eat in Grand Central Station?
A hamburger ☐ **Oysters** ☐ **Steak and salad** ☐

To: Sam
Subject: Trip to New York

Hi Sam,
We're having a great time in New York. There's so much to do. We arrived on Friday and went up the Empire State Building. Then, on Saturday, we took the boat to Staten Island and saw the Statue of Liberty. I was surprised because it looked quite small. Yesterday, I went to a store called Macy's and bought some nice clothes. Then we went to a famous restaurant in Grand Central Station and ate oysters.

Love from Sue xx

29.11 SAY THE QUESTIONS OUT LOUD, FILLING IN THE GAPS

When _did you visit China_ ?
We visited China in 2011.

3 What _____ ?
We ate fried rice in Chinatown.

1 Who _____ ?
I went on vacation with Jo.

4 How _____ for?
We went abroad for six months.

2 Where _____ ?
We stayed in a hotel in London.

5 When _____ ?
We left the US on June 29th.

---

29 ✓ CHECKLIST

⚙ Past simple questions ☐   **Aa** Travel and activities ☐   🧩 Talking about vacations ☐

30 Applying for a job

If you want to find a job, you need to understand the English words and phrases used in advertisements and on recruitment websites.

⚙ **New language** Interview responses
Aa Vocabulary Job words and phrases
🧩 **New skill** Dealing with job applications

30.1 VOCABULARY APPLYING FOR A JOB

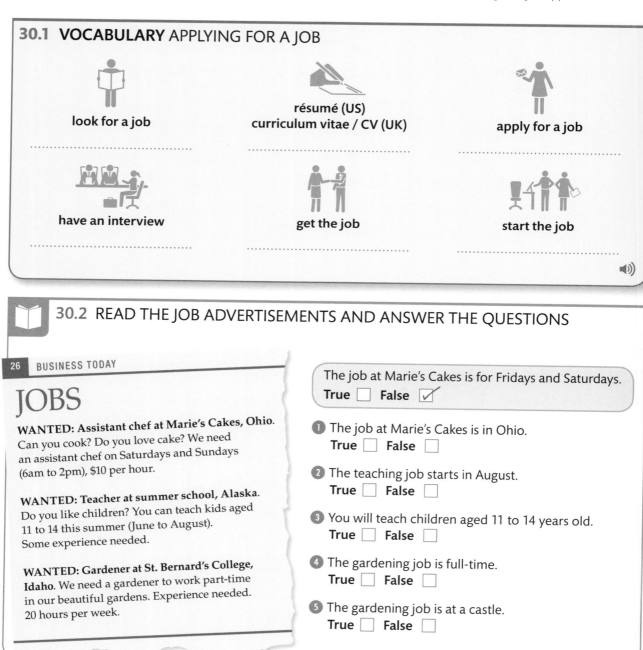

look for a job

résumé (US)
curriculum vitae / CV (UK)

apply for a job

have an interview

get the job

start the job

🔊

30.2 READ THE JOB ADVERTISEMENTS AND ANSWER THE QUESTIONS

26 **BUSINESS TODAY**

JOBS

WANTED: Assistant chef at Marie's Cakes, Ohio.
Can you cook? Do you love cake? We need an assistant chef on Saturdays and Sundays (6am to 2pm), $10 per hour.

WANTED: Teacher at summer school, Alaska.
Do you like children? You can teach kids aged 11 to 14 this summer (June to August). Some experience needed.

WANTED: Gardener at St. Bernard's College, Idaho. We need a gardener to work part-time in our beautiful gardens. Experience needed. 20 hours per week.

The job at Marie's Cakes is for Fridays and Saturdays.
True ☐ **False** ☑

① The job at Marie's Cakes is in Ohio.
True ☐ **False** ☐

② The teaching job starts in August.
True ☐ **False** ☐

③ You will teach children aged 11 to 14 years old.
True ☐ **False** ☐

④ The gardening job is full-time.
True ☐ **False** ☐

⑤ The gardening job is at a castle.
True ☐ **False** ☐

30.3 VOCABULARY WORDS IN YOUR RÉSUMÉ

qualification   work experience   hobby   interest   reference

Aa   30.4 FILL IN THE GAPS USING THE WORDS IN THE PANEL

I need to give the interviewer a ___*reference*___ from my last boss.

1. My _____ include degrees in biology and chemistry.

2. The interview at the bank went really well. I've _____ .

3. The manager read my _____ and said it was really good.

4. I can _____ the job in January.

5. You need to _____ before you can get the job.

| have an interview | ~~reference~~ | qualifications | résumé | got the job | start |

30.5 LISTEN TO THE AUDIO, THEN NUMBER THE QUESTIONS IN THE ORDER THAT YOU HEAR THEM

Tom Willis is being interviewed for a job.

A Why do you want this job? ☐   D When can you start work? ☐

B What did you do at the store? ☐   E Why did you leave the music store? ☐

C Why did you study English at college? 1   F Are you good at working with people? ☐

30 ✓ CHECKLIST

⚙ Interview responses ☐   **Aa** Job words and phrases ☐   🧩 Dealing with job applications ☐

There are two kinds of question: subject questions and object questions. You form them in different ways in order to ask about different things.

⚙ **New language** Subject and object questions
Aa Vocabulary Workplace words
🧩 **New skill** Asking different kinds of question

31.1 KEY LANGUAGE OBJECT QUESTIONS

Use object questions to ask who received an action, not who did the action. They are called object questions because the question word is the object of the main verb.

Object — Who **did you** see at lunchtime? — Subject

Use the auxiliary "did" as with normal questions.

I **saw my boss.**

The answer is the object of the question.

31.2 FURTHER EXAMPLES OBJECT QUESTIONS

What **did he eat?**

He **ate** steak and salad.

Who **did you speak to?**

I **spoke to** Jane.

31.3 HOW TO FORM OBJECT QUESTIONS

OBJECT	AUXILIARY	SUBJECT	VERB
What	did	he	eat?
Who	did	you	see?

Different question words can be used here.

The auxiliary tells you whether the question is talking about the past or the present.

31.4 VOCABULARY IN THE WORKPLACE

customer

boss

manager

salary

pay

staff

company

nine-to-five job

part-time

full-time

31.5 LISTEN AND MARK AS TRUE OR FALSE

Gemma and Arjun are talking about where they work.

Gemma likes her manager.
True ☐ False ☑

① Gemma doesn't work in an office now.
True ☐ False ☐

② Arjun wants a higher salary.
True ☐ False ☐

③ They like working from 9am to 5pm.
True ☐ False ☐

④ Gemma is going on vacation in October.
True ☐ False ☐

⑤ Arjun likes talking to the customers.
True ☐ False ☐

31.6 WRITE OBJECT QUESTIONS TO MATCH THE STATEMENTS

I had lunch with my boss on Monday.
Who _did you have lunch with on Monday?_

① Sharon got a new job yesterday.
What _____

② My boss had a meeting this morning.
What _____

③ I want a higher salary.
What _____

④ The staff phoned all our customers last month.
Who _____

⑤ I saw my manager on TV last night.
Who _____

31.7 KEY LANGUAGE SUBJECT QUESTIONS

Use subject questions to ask who did the action. They are called subject questions because the question word is the subject of the main verb.

Subject ⟶ Ben **called** the bank. ⟵ Object

SUBJECT QUESTION

Question doesn't use "did." ⟶

Who **called** the bank?

Ben.

OBJECT QUESTION

Question uses "did." ⟶

Who **did** Ben **call**?

The bank.

31.8 FURTHER EXAMPLES SUBJECT AND OBJECT QUESTIONS

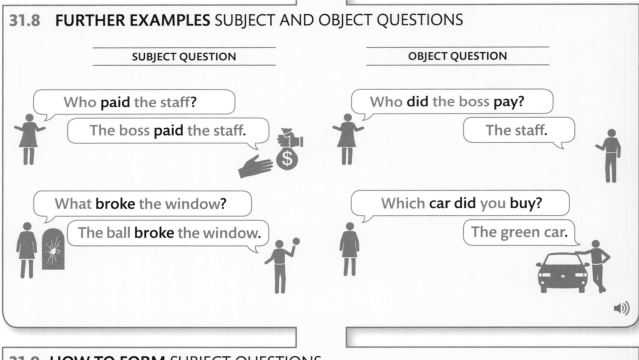

SUBJECT QUESTION

Who **paid** the staff?

The boss **paid** the staff.

What **broke** the window?

The ball **broke** the window.

OBJECT QUESTION

Who **did** the boss **pay**?

The staff.

Which **car did** you **buy**?

The green car.

31.9 HOW TO FORM SUBJECT QUESTIONS

"Who" is the most common pronoun used in subject questions, but you might hear others.

SUBJECT	VERB	OBJECT
Who	called	the bank?

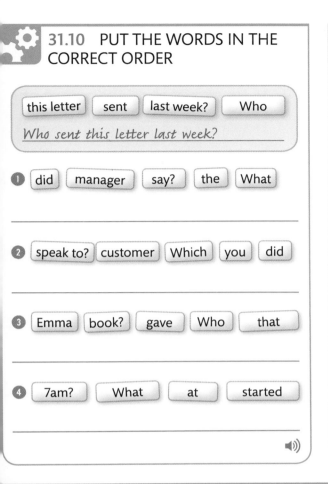

31.10 PUT THE WORDS IN THE CORRECT ORDER

this letter | sent | last week? | Who

Who sent this letter last week?

1. did | manager | say? | the | What

_____

2. speak to? | customer | Which | you | did

_____

3. Emma | book? | gave | Who | that

_____

4. 7am? | What | at | started

_____

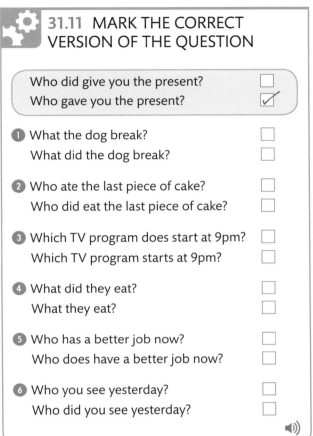

31.11 MARK THE CORRECT VERSION OF THE QUESTION

Who did give you the present? ☐
Who gave you the present? ☑

1. What the dog break? ☐
   What did the dog break? ☐

2. Who ate the last piece of cake? ☐
   Who did eat the last piece of cake? ☐

3. Which TV program does start at 9pm? ☐
   Which TV program starts at 9pm? ☐

4. What did they eat? ☐
   What they eat? ☐

5. Who has a better job now? ☐
   Who does have a better job now? ☐

6. Who you see yesterday? ☐
   Who did you see yesterday? ☐

31.12 WRITE QUESTIONS TO MATCH THE STATEMENTS

His old manager paid him a higher salary.
Who *paid him a higher salary?*

1. Arjun started a full-time job last month.

   What _____

2. The office has a new door.

   What _____

3. The customers are waiting outside.

   Who _____

4. Mark wants to be a teacher.

   What _____

5. The boss wants a new office this year.

   What _____

---

31 ✓ CHECKLIST

⚙ Subject and object questions ☐   **Aa** Workplace words ☐   🧩 Asking different kinds of question ☐

32 Someone, anyone, everyone

Use indefinite pronouns, such as "anyone," "someone,"
and "everyone," to refer to a person or a group of people
without explaining who they are.

🔧 **New language** Indefinite pronouns
Aa Vocabulary Office words
🧩 **New skill** Talking about people in general

32.1 KEY LANGUAGE "ANYONE / SOMEONE"

Use "someone" or "somebody" to refer to a person in a positive statement, and "anyone" or "anybody" for a question or a negative statement.

You can also use "anybody." Both words mean: any person.

 Did anyone call me this morning?

Yes, someone called you at 11 o'clock.

You can also use "somebody." Both words mean: a person.

🔊

32.2 FURTHER EXAMPLES "ANYONE / SOMEONE"

Someone is working late.

Somebody left this letter on my desk.

Did anyone buy a gift for Mrs. Tan?

I didn't give anybody your name.

The statement is negative, so use "anybody/anyone."

🔊

 ## 32.3 CROSS OUT THE INCORRECT WORD IN EACH SENTENCE

I saw ~~anyone~~ / someone at reception this morning.

❶ Please ask anyone / someone to phone Mr. Richards immediately.

❷ Mrs. Turner didn't give anyone / someone any work to do this week.

❸ Can I give anyone / someone a lift to the station tomorrow morning?

❹ Mr. Phillips needs anyone / someone to go with him to the hospital.

❺ I'm sorry, but there isn't anyone / someone in the office at the moment.

🔊

32.4 KEY LANGUAGE "EVERYONE / NO ONE"

Use "everyone" or "everybody" to refer to the whole group in a statement or question. "No one" or "nobody" means none of the group.

"No one" is written as two words.

Why is there no one in the office?

Everyone is at the big meeting.

Use the singular form of the verb after "everyone" and "everybody."

32.5 LISTEN TO THE AUDIO AND CROSS OUT THE INCORRECT WORD IN EACH SENTENCE

~~Everybody~~ / Somebody wants to have a meeting this afternoon.

1 Nobody / Somebody in room 212 needs a new computer.

2 Theodore tells everyone / someone the good news about the business.

3 Everyone / Anybody is going for lunch at the restaurant to celebrate Daniella's birthday.

4 Nobody / Somebody closed the window last night before they left the office.

5 Everyone / Anyone knows that we have a new office.

32.6 USE THE CHART TO CREATE 12 CORRECT SENTENCES AND SAY THEM OUT LOUD

Everybody went to the meeting.

| Everybody Someone Nobody | went to wrote to finished | the meeting. the party. the customer. their work today. |

---

32 ✓ CHECKLIST

⚙ Indefinite pronouns ☐   **Aa** Office words ☐   🧩 Talking about people in general ☐

33 Making conversation

Short questions are a way of showing interest when you are talking with someone. Use them to keep the conversation going.

⚙ **New language** Short questions
Aa Vocabulary Question words
🧩 **New skill** Asking short questions

33.1 KEY LANGUAGE SHORT QUESTIONS

You already know the answers to short questions. Use them to invite the person speaking to say more.

For many verbs, use the auxiliary verb "do" to form the question.

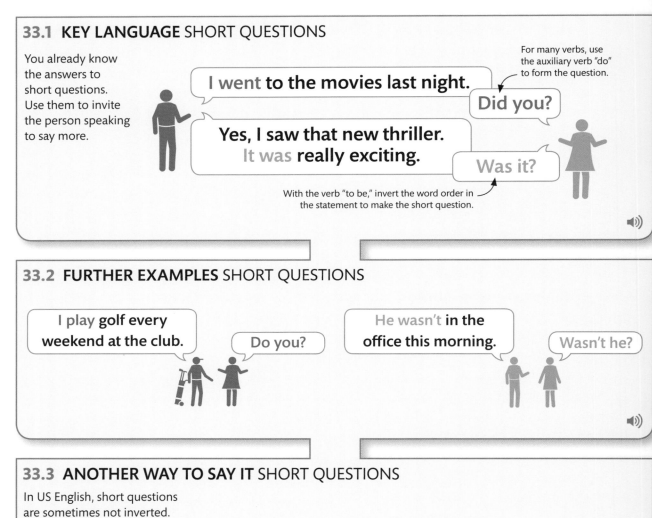

I went **to the movies last night.**

Did you?

Yes, I saw that new thriller. It was **really exciting.**

Was it?

With the verb "to be," invert the word order in the statement to make the short question.

33.2 FURTHER EXAMPLES SHORT QUESTIONS

I play **golf every weekend at the club.**

Do you?

He wasn't **in the office this morning.**

Wasn't he?

33.3 ANOTHER WAY TO SAY IT SHORT QUESTIONS

In US English, short questions are sometimes not inverted.

They didn't go **to the theater last night.**

They didn't?

There isn't **any milk left in the fridge.**

There isn't?

33.4 MATCH THE STATEMENTS TO THE SHORT QUESTIONS

Laura went paragliding. —→ She did?

Didn't you?

1 I was very tired last night.

2 We didn't go to the party.

Does it?

3 Frank wasn't feeling well.

Were you?

4 The cat likes its new food.

He wasn't?

🔊

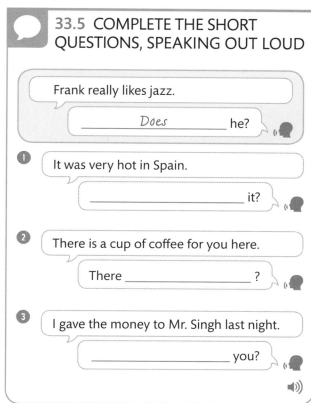

33.5 COMPLETE THE SHORT QUESTIONS, SPEAKING OUT LOUD

Frank really likes jazz.

_____ *Does* _____ he?

1 It was very hot in Spain.

_____ it?

2 There is a cup of coffee for you here.

There _____ ?

3 I gave the money to Mr. Singh last night.

_____ you?

🔊

33 ✓ CHECKLIST

⚙ Short questions ☐   **Aa** Question words ☐   🧩 Asking short questions ☐

🔁 REVIEW THE ENGLISH YOU HAVE LEARNED IN UNITS 29-33

NEW LANGUAGE	SAMPLE SENTENCE	☑	UNIT
QUESTIONS IN THE PAST SIMPLE	"Did you have a good vacation?" "Yes, we went to India."	☐	29.1, 29.3, 29.7
SUBJECT AND OBJECT QUESTIONS	Who called the bank? Who did Ben call?	☐	31.1, 31.7, 31.8
"SOMEONE" AND "ANYONE"	"Did anyone call me this morning?" "Yes, someone called at 11 o'clock."	☐	32.1, 32.2
"EVERYONE" AND "NO ONE"	"Why is there no one in the office?" "Everyone is at the big meeting."	☐	32.4
SHORT QUESTIONS	"I went to the movies last night." "Did you?" "It was really exciting." "Was it?"	☐	33.1, 33.2

34 Vocabulary

34.1 GOING OUT

art gallery

book club

night club

concert hall

fun fair

circus

restaurant

bar

menu

waiter

waitress

check (US)
bill (UK)

ballet

opera

band

orchestra

musician

festival

concert

show

audience

applause

meet friends

go clubbing

go dancing

go to a party

go to a restaurant

go to the movies (US)
go to the cinema (UK)

see a play

do karaoke

go bowling

buy a ticket

35 Future arrangements

You can use the present continuous to talk about things that are happening now. You can also use it to talk about arrangements for the future.

⚙ **New language** Future with present continuous
Aa Vocabulary Excuses
🧩 **New skill** Talking about future arrangements

35.1 KEY LANGUAGE PRESENT CONTINUOUS WITH FUTURE EVENTS

Use time phrases to show whether a verb in the present continuous refers to the present or the future.

"At the moment" refers to the present.

Present continuous refers to Dave's present activity.

 At the moment Dave is working, but tomorrow he is playing golf.

Time clause "tomorrow" refers to the future.

Present continuous refers to a future event that is planned.

35.2 FURTHER EXAMPLES PRESENT CONTINUOUS WITH FUTURE EVENTS

 Jack's playing soccer now, then later he's seeing a movie.

 Sue is studying now, but this evening she's visiting a friend.

 Today, **I'm playing tennis, but I'm playing golf tomorrow.**

You can use the time word or phrase at the start or end of a clause.

 I'm reading at the moment, **but I'm going running later.**

35.3 KEY LANGUAGE "ON / IN" WITH DAYS, MONTHS, AND DATES

Use the preposition "on" in front of days of the week and specific dates. Use "in" with months and years.

I'm working on Tuesday.

I'm working on May 9th.

I'm retiring in June.

I'm retiring in 2035.

35.4 FILL IN THE GAPS BY PUTTING THE VERBS IN THE PRESENT CONTINUOUS

I _____ *am watching* _____ (watch) TV with my friends tonight.

1 John's cousins _____ (come) to the party tomorrow.

2 I _____ (go) to the dentist tomorrow morning.

3 My family and I _____ (visit) my grandma on Saturday.

4 The managers in my office _____ (have) a meeting this afternoon.

5 A famous band _____ (play) in Central Park this weekend.

6 He _____ (study) for his test tomorrow.

35.5 LISTEN TO THE AUDIO, THEN NUMBER THE PICTURES IN THE ORDER YOU HEAR THEM

A ☐   B ☐   C 1   D ☐

E ☐   F ☐   G ☐

35.6 KEY LANGUAGE MAKING EXCUSES

Sometimes you need to say why you can't do something. To be polite, use an expression like "Sorry, I can't" before saying what your other plans are.

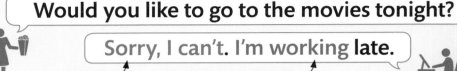

Would you like to go to the movies tonight?

Sorry, I can't. I'm working **late.**

To be polite, apologize first.

Use the present continuous to say what you are doing instead.

35.7 FURTHER EXAMPLES MAKING EXCUSES

I'd like to, but I'm going **to the dentist.**

I'd love to, but I'm meeting **friends.**

That would be fun, but I'm visiting **family.**

That sounds nice, but I'm playing **baseball.**

35.8 REWRITE THE SENTENCES, PUTTING THE WORDS IN THE CORRECT ORDER

| tonight. | fun, but | theater | That | the | I'm | going to | would be |

That would be fun, but I'm going to the theater tonight.

1 | my | parents | I'm | Sorry, I can't. | visiting | this | evening. |

_____

2 | this | like to, | but | weekend. | I'd | France | going to | I'm |

_____

3 | sounds | but | I'm going | That | on Tuesday. | nice, | swimming |

_____

4 | love to, | I'm | looking after | I'd | my nephew | tomorrow. | but |

_____

35.9 ANSWER EACH INVITATION OUT LOUD, USING AN EXCUSE FROM THE DIARY

September 2020

21 SATURDAY

9am – Play soccer with Eva.

Noon – Go to lunch with Aziz.

1:30–3pm – Look after Sandy's baby.

4pm – Go to yoga class.

6pm – Go to dinner with Marco and Olivia.

7:30pm – Go to the theater to see a musical.

Would you like to come swimming at 9am?

I'd love to, but ___I'm playing soccer with Eva.___

3 Would you like to play tennis at 7:30pm?

That would be fun, but_____ _____

1 Would you like to come to dinner tonight?

I'd like to, but_____ _____

4 Would you like to go shopping at 2pm?

That sounds nice, but_____ _____

2 Would you like to go to lunch today?

Sorry, I can't._____ _____

5 Would you like to go to a dance class at 4pm?

I'd like to, but_____ _____

35 ✓ CHECKLIST

⚙ Future with present continuous ☐   **Aa** Excuses ☐   🧩 Talking about future arrangements ☐

117

36 Plans and intentions

You can use "going to" to talk about what you want to do in the future. Use it also to talk about specific plans, such as when and where you're going to do something.

🗝️ **New language** Future tense
Aa Vocabulary Time words and phrases
New skill Talking about your plans

36.1 KEY LANGUAGE "GOING TO" FOR FUTURE PLANS

Use the verb "to be" with "going to" to say what you plan to do.

Base form of verb.

I'm going to buy a new car.

We are going to cook dinner tonight.

"Going to" doesn't change with the subject.

Use a time word or time phrase to say when you will cook dinner.

36.2 FURTHER EXAMPLES "GOING TO" FOR FUTURE PLANS

I'm going to start this book soon.

Sam's going to get fit before his next birthday.

We're going to cycle from Boston to Cape Cod next weekend.

I'm not going to eat any chocolate this month.

Add "not" after the verb "to be" to make the negative.

36.3 HOW TO FORM "GOING TO" FOR FUTURE PLANS

SUBJECT	"TO BE"	"GOING TO"	BASE FORM OF VERB	REST OF SENTENCE
He	is	going to	buy	a new car.

36.4 FILL IN THE GAPS PUTTING THE VERBS IN THE FUTURE WITH "GOING TO"

Darren and Miki ___*are going to watch*___ (🚶🚶 watch) a movie tonight.

1 I _____ (🍽️ not eat) sushi for dinner.

2 Debra _____ (🤝 get) a new job soon.

3 My friends _____ (👩‍🍳 cook) a meal for me next week.

4 Manuel _____ (🤿 learn) how to scuba dive this summer.

5 We _____ (🧳✈️ travel) to Dubai in December.

🔊

36.5 READ THE ARTICLE AND ANSWER THE QUESTIONS

4 The Weekly You

WHAT ARE YOUR RESOLUTIONS?

Exercise more or stop eating chocolate? It's a question many of us ask ourselves as the year ends.

Betty from California makes one resolution every year. "I'm not going to give up smoking," she tells us, "because I did that last time. This year, I'm going to get fit!"

In the US only 8 percent of people keep to their resolutions. Many give up by the end of January.

A lot of people make resolutions, but Australian Joanna Gee makes one resolution for every day of the year. That's 365 resolutions every year.

"I love making resolutions," Joanna says. "This year I'm going to do more unusual things. On June 23 I'm going to climb a mountain, and then on September 30 I'm going to swim with sharks."

Betty has one resolution this year.
True ✓ **False** ☐

1 Betty is going to give up smoking this year.
True ☐ **False** ☐

2 Only 8% of Americans keep to their resolutions.
True ☐ **False** ☐

3 Joanna has a resolution for every day of the year.
True ☐ **False** ☐

4 Joanna is going to climb a mountain on July 23.
True ☐ **False** ☐

5 Joanna is going to swim with dolphins.
True ☐ **False** ☐

36.6 KEY LANGUAGE "BY" WITH TIME WORDS AND PHRASES

"By" followed by a noun or time phrase means something will happen at some point before that time.

"Going to" follows the verb "to be."

I am going to paint the house by June.

NOW   JUNE

36.7 FURTHER EXAMPLES "BY" WITH TIME WORDS AND PHRASES

You are going to write to the person between now and next weekend.

I am going to write to you by next weekend.

I am going to get fit by this time next year.

You are going to get fit by the same date the following year.

36.8 READ JACK'S RESOLUTIONS, THEN WRITE ABOUT THEM USING "GOING TO"

> He is going to tidy his house by the weekend.

Jack's January Resolutions

- Tidy my house by the weekend.
- Paint my bedroom by the end of this month.
- Join a gym by this time next month.
- Book a vacation by the end of March.
- Get fit by the summer.
- Buy a new car by December.

1 _____

2 _____

3 _____

4 _____

5 _____

36.9 REWRITE THE SENTENCES, PUTTING THE WORDS IN THE CORRECT ORDER

| end of | are | next year. | Aziz and Julie | get married | going to | by the |

Aziz and Julie are going to get married by the end of next year.

❶ | by | going to | buy | Tim | a | October. | is | new boat |

❷ | are | going to | on the | Sally and Jane | vacation | go on | weekend. |

❸ | next year. | by | going to | write | a book | I am | this time |

❹ | run | are | tomorrow. | a | marathon | going to | We |

36.10 LISTEN TO THE AUDIO, THEN MATCH EACH PERSON TO THE CORRECT ACTIVITY AND TIME PHRASE

Tom	is going to join a gym	by December.
❶ Jack	is going to write music	in the winter.
❷ Samantha	is going to buy a new car	by this time next month.
❸ Debbie	is going to learn how to cook	before the summer.
❹ Joseph	is going to travel more	at weekends.

36 ✓ CHECKLIST

⚙ Future tense ☐ **Aa** Time words and phrases ☐ 🧩 Talking about your plans ☐

37 What's going to happen

Use the future with "going to" to make a prediction about the future when there is evidence in the present moment to back up that prediction.

⚙️ **New language** The future with "going to"

Aa Vocabulary Prediction verbs

🧩 **New skill** Predicting future events

37.1 KEY LANGUAGE "GOING TO" FOR FUTURE EVENTS

This form of the future is formed using "to be" + "going to" + the base form of the verb.

Use "going to" to give your prediction.

Look at those clouds. It's going to rain soon.

Evidence in the present moment means that you can make a prediction.

🔊

37.2 FURTHER EXAMPLES "GOING TO" FOR FUTURE EVENTS

Oh no! She's going to slip and fall over.

The hill is too steep. Jon is going to crash!

She studies a lot. She's going to pass her exam.

Look! The waiter is going to drop those plates.

They're going to break a window.

Joe fell asleep in the exam. He's going to fail.

He's wearing a raincoat, so he's not going to get wet.

 🔊

37.3 FILL IN THE GAPS PUTTING THE VERBS IN THE FUTURE WITH "GOING TO"

Kim doesn't study very hard. She _____*is going to fail*_____ (☒ fail) her exams.

1 Watch out! You _____ (step into) that puddle.

2 The dog _____ (not eat) its food. I think it's sick.

3 Oh no! She _____ (fall off) the ladder.

4 John is terrible at golf! He _____ (not win) the tournament.

5 It's very windy! His umbrella _____ (blow away).

6 You're carrying too much. You _____ (drop) everything.

37.4 REWRITE THE SENTENCES, CORRECTING THE ERRORS

The traffic is moving very slowly. I **are** going to be late for work.
The traffic is moving very slowly. I am going to be late for work.

1 John and Jill are putting their coats on. They **is** going to leave now.

_____

2 I saw the weather forecast. It **are** going to snow this afternoon.

_____

3 It's my birthday, so I **is** going to get a present from my husband.

_____

4 Larry and John have gone home to get their tennis rackets. They **is** going to play tennis.

_____

37.5 READ THE SCHOOL REPORT, THEN FILL IN THE GAPS USING "GOING TO" OR "NOT GOING TO"

Report: Marco Di Stefano

Marco is ___going to___ pass his history exam.

❶ He is _____ be in the next Olympics.

❷ Marco is _____ study art at college.

❸ He is _____ be the main character in a musical.

❹ Marco is _____ fail his English exam.

❺ He is _____ play soccer next weekend.

English 33%	Marco needs to work harder at Englis He is predicted not to pass this exam.
History 95%	This is Marco's best subject. He doesn have any problems and will do well in the exam.
Music 25%	Marco doesn't like to sing and doesn't play a musical instrument.
Art 92%	Marco loves this subject and is very good at it. He has an offer from Rome Art College and wants to study art.
Gym 55%	This is not Marco's best subject, but he is a member of the soccer team. They play every weekend.

Aa 37.6 READ THE CLUES AND WRITE THE ANSWERS IN THE CORRECT PLACES ON THE GRID

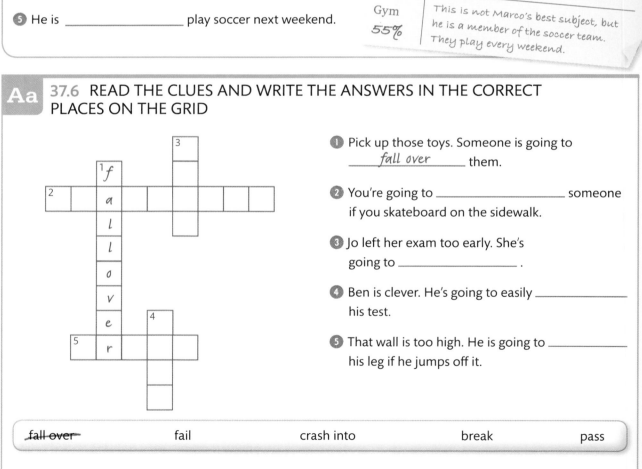

❶ Pick up those toys. Someone is going to ___fall over___ them.

❷ You're going to _____ someone if you skateboard on the sidewalk.

❸ Jo left her exam too early. She's going to _____ .

❹ Ben is clever. He's going to easily _____ his test.

❺ That wall is too high. He is going to _____ his leg if he jumps off it.

fall over   fail   crash into   break   pass

124

37.7 LOOK AT THE PICTURES, THEN FILL IN THE GAPS USING THE WORDS IN THE PANEL, SPEAKING OUT LOUD

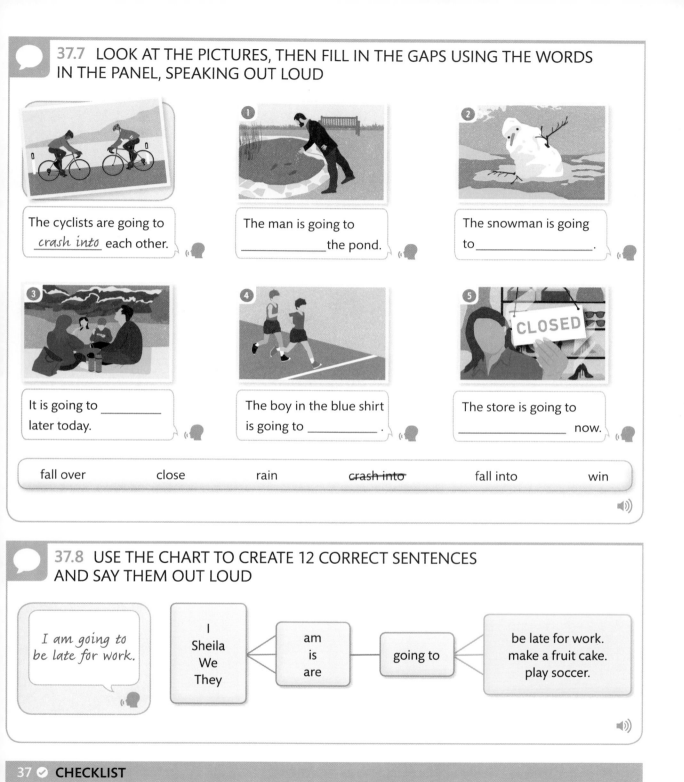

The cyclists are going to _crash into_ each other.

① The man is going to _____ the pond.

② The snowman is going to _____.

③ It is going to _____ later today.

④ The boy in the blue shirt is going to _____.

⑤ The store is going to _____ now.

| fall over | close | rain | crash into | fall into | win |

37.8 USE THE CHART TO CREATE 12 CORRECT SENTENCES AND SAY THEM OUT LOUD

I am going to be late for work.

| I / Sheila / We / They | am / is / are | going to | be late for work. / make a fruit cake. / play soccer. |

38 Vocabulary

38.1 ANIMALS

insect

fish

bird

bear

rhino

buffalo

camel

lion

tiger

elephant

monkey

giraffe

kangaroo

bull

cow

mouse

rat

eagle

snake

lizard

frog

shark

whale

dolphin

crab

octopus

turtle

crocodile

bee

fly

spider

butterfly

39 Making predictions

You can use the verb "will" to talk about future events in English. This form of the future tense has a slightly different meaning from futures using "going to."

⚙ **New language** The future with "will"
Aa **Vocabulary** Prediction words
🧩 **New skill** Saying what you think will happen

39.1 KEY LANGUAGE THE FUTURE WITH "WILL"

Use "will" to say what you think will happen in the future when you don't have firm evidence for your prediction.

That new movie is great. They will love it.

You think the other people will love the movie, but you don't have firm evidence.

39.2 FURTHER EXAMPLES THE FUTURE WITH "WILL"

 Jane will like the new house. It's really nice.

 It'll rain every day this summer.

You can also say "he'll not," but "won't" is more common in US English.

In negative sentences, "not" goes between "will" and the base form of the verb.

 We will not get home before midnight.

 He won't be late for work again this year.

In spoken English, you normally use the contracted form of "will."

 They'll enjoy their holiday in Venice.

 She'll be really angry when she finds out.

39.3 HOW TO FORM THE FUTURE WITH "WILL"

"Will" is a modal verb, so its form doesn't change with the subject.

SUBJECT	"WILL"	BASE FORM OF VERB	REST OF SENTENCE
She	will	love	the new movie.

39.4 FILL IN THE GAPS USING THE FUTURE WITH "WILL" OR "WILL NOT"

You _____ will love _____ (love) my new sweater.

❶ John _____ (not eat) pizza.

❷ Maria _____ (enjoy) the new dance class.

❸ Susie and Bella _____ (be) early for work this week.

❹ The children _____ (not understand) this information.

39.5 READ THE NOTE AND REWRITE THE HIGHLIGHTED PHRASES USING PRONOUNS AND CONTRACTED "WILL" WITH FUTURE VERBS

He'll buy pizzas.

❶ _____

❷ _____

❸ _____

❹ _____

❺ _____

Hi Jim,
What do you want us to bring to movie night? Ben will buy pizzas because he always does. John will bring chocolates and Mary will make a salad. As usual, David won't bring anything. I will bring drinks, and Lillian and Jo will buy cheese.
Is that OK?
Sandy

39.6 LISTEN TO THE AUDIO AND MATCH THE QUESTIONS TO THE CORRECT ANSWERS

Who will clean the house? → Jenny's sister will do it.

❶ Who will find the party music?   Jenny's brother will do it.

❷ Who will bring the party games?   Jenny's mother will do it.

❸ Who will bake a birthday cake?   Sam will do it.

❹ Who will cook the food?   Marsha will do it.

39.7 KEY LANGUAGE "THINK" WITH "WILL"

If you're not sure about something, you can begin a sentence with "I think." This shows you are giving your opinion.

You're not certain.

"That" is not essential to the sentence, and it's often left out.

We think that he'll like the play.

39.8 HOW TO FORM "THINK" WITH "WILL"

SUBJECT	"THINK"	"THAT"	SUBJECT + "WILL"	VERB	REST OF SENTENCE
We	think	**that**	he'll	**like**	**the play.**

"That" is often left out.

39.9 FURTHER EXAMPLES SENTENCES WITH "THINK" AND "WILL"

I think that we'll have enough food for the party.

He thinks it'll be a great show tonight.

It's cold outside, but we don't think it'll snow today.

To make the sentence negative, add "do not" or "don't" before "think."

She doesn't think she'll get that job at the bank.

39.10 MATCH THE SENTENCES TO THE CORRECT PREDICTIONS

Max cooks great meals at home. ——→ I think he'll become a fantastic chef.

1. Diana works very hard.
2. Chiara loves traveling.
3. Carl failed his driver's test again.
4. Georgia can't sing very well.

I think she'll pass her exams.

I don't think she'll be in the musical.

I think he'll become a fantastic chef.

I think she'll enjoy visiting Rome.

I don't think he'll ever pass it.

39.11 KEY LANGUAGE "GOING TO" AND "WILL"

Use "going to" when you have evidence for a prediction. Use "will" when a prediction is an opinion without evidence.

You are predicting this, but you don't have firm evidence.

I think Number 5 will win.

Look, Number 5 is going to win.

You are predicting this based on firm evidence.

39.12 LOOK AT THE PICTURES, THEN SAY THE SENTENCES OUT LOUD, FILLING IN THE GAPS USING THE PHRASES IN THE PANEL

Lily is going to ___*jump*___ the fence.

❶ Bob is going to _____ all his dinner.

❷ It is going to _____ this afternoon.

❸ The dog will _____ these leftovers.

❹ The car is going to _____ left.

❺ John thinks he will _____ tonight.

eat	~~jump~~	turn	go out	eat	snow

---

39 ✓ CHECKLIST

⚙ The future with "will" ☐   **Aa** Prediction words ☐   🧩 Saying what you think will happen ☐

40 Making quick decisions

You can use "will" to talk about the future in two ways: when you make a prediction without evidence, and when you make a quick decision to do something.

⚙ **New language** Quick decisions with "will"
Aa **Vocabulary** Decision words
🧩 **New skill** Talking about future actions

40.1 KEY LANGUAGE QUICK DECISIONS WITH "WILL"

If you suddenly decide to do something while you're speaking, use "will" to say what you're going to do.

Oh, it's raining!
I'll take my umbrella.

"Will" shows you have just made the decision.

40.2 FURTHER EXAMPLES QUICK DECISIONS WITH "WILL"

Contracted form of "will not."

It's midnight, so I won't walk home through the park.

This apple is delicious. I'll have another one.

40.3 KEY LANGUAGE "SO / IN THAT CASE"

Use "so" or the expression "in that case" to link a situation and the decision you make as a result of that situation.

SITUATION   DECISION

 There's no juice, so I'll have water.

 The car won't start. In that case we'll walk.

SITUATION   DECISION

40.4 MATCH THE BEGINNINGS OF THE SENTENCES TO THE CORRECT ENDINGS

There's no bread, — so I'll go to the supermarket.

so I won't go in the water.

1 It's my birthday, — so I won't go shopping.

2 I forgot my swimming trunks, — so I'll get the bus.

3 I don't have any money,

4 I can't find my train ticket, — so I'll cut the cake.

40.5 LISTEN TO THE AUDIO, THEN NUMBER THE PICTURES IN THE ORDER THEY ARE DESCRIBED

A ☐
B ☐
C 1
D ☐
E ☐

40.6 FILL IN THE GAPS USING THE WORDS IN THE PANEL

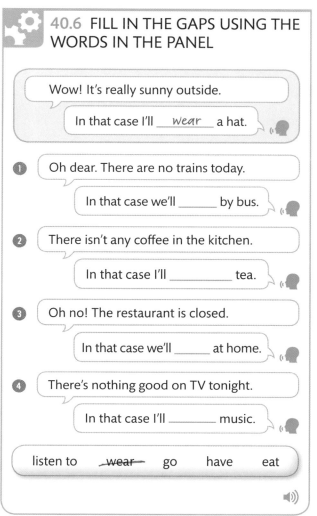

Wow! It's really sunny outside.

In that case I'll __wear__ a hat.

1 Oh dear. There are no trains today.

In that case we'll _____ by bus.

2 There isn't any coffee in the kitchen.

In that case I'll _____ tea.

3 Oh no! The restaurant is closed.

In that case we'll _____ at home.

4 There's nothing good on TV tonight.

In that case I'll _____ music.

listen to   ~~wear~~   go   have   eat

40.7 KEY LANGUAGE "THINK" WITH "WILL"

You can use "think" with "will" to show that your decision is something you are considering.

I'm tired. I think I'll go to bed.

You are deciding now.
You're not completely sure.

40.8 FURTHER EXAMPLES "THINK" WITH "WILL"

There are lots of options on the menu. I think we'll have the fish.

There are lots of bands to see, but I think I'll watch the rock band.

This movie is terrible. I think I'll leave before the end.

It's getting really hot outside. I think I'll put my shorts on.

40.9 READ THE TEXT MESSAGES AND ANSWER THE QUESTIONS

Two friends will buy her flowers.
True ☐   False ☑

1 One friend will take her to a restaurant.
True ☐   False ☐

2 One friend will have a party for her.
True ☐   False ☐

3 One friend will get her ballet tickets.
True ☐   False ☐

4 Two friends will take her shopping.
True ☐   False ☐

5 One friend will make her a birthday cake.
True ☐   False ☐

6 One friend will buy her a DVD.
True ☐   False ☐

> **Jo**
>
> It's Jeanie's birthday this weekend. Do you know what we can do for her, Sally?
>
> Sure, Jo. I think I'll get her some flowers and a DVD.
>
> Great. I think I'll take her shopping and buy her some clothes. What will James do?
>
> James will have a party for her at his house on Tuesday.
>
> Perfect. John will cook the food and bake her a cake.
>
> Oh, and I think Jemima will buy Jeanie some movie tickets and take her shopping.

40.10 SAY THE SENTENCES OUT LOUD, FILLING IN THE GAPS USING THE PHRASES IN THE PANEL

The TV is broken. What will you do tonight?

I think I'll ___read a book___.

1 There's no juice. What do you want to drink?

I think I'll _____.

2 What time are you leaving work?

I think I'll _____.

3 Jo is busy, so who will you play tennis with?

I think I'll _____.

4 Which TV show do you want to see?

I think I'll _____.

5 Where do you want to go now?

I think I'll _____.

play with Cassie   have milk   ~~read a book~~   leave at 6:30pm   go home   watch the news

---

40 ✓ CHECKLIST

⚙️ Quick decisions with "will" ☐   **Aa** Decision words ☐   🧩 Talking about future actions ☐

🔄 REVIEW THE ENGLISH YOU HAVE LEARNED IN UNITS 35–40

NEW LANGUAGE	SAMPLE SENTENCE	✓	UNIT
FUTURE TENSE WITH PRESENT CONTINUOUS	At the moment, Dave is working, but tomorrow he is playing golf.	☐	35.1, 35.3, 35.6
"GOING TO" FOR FUTURE PLANS	I'm going to buy a new car. We are going to exercise tonight.	☐	36.1, 36.6
FUTURE TENSE WITH "GOING TO"	Look at those clouds. It's going to rain soon.	☐	37.1, 37.2
FUTURE TENSE WITH "WILL"	That new movie is great. They will love it.	☐	39.1, 39.7, 39.11
QUICK DECISIONS WITH "WILL"	Oh, it's raining! I'll take my umbrella.	☐	40.1, 40.2, 40.7

41 Future possibilities

Use "might" to show you're not sure if you'll do something. It's a possibility and you don't want to say that you "will" or you "won't."

⚙ **New language** Using "might"
Aa Vocabulary Activities, food, and pastimes
🧩 **New skill** Talking about future possibilities

41.1 KEY LANGUAGE "MIGHT" WITH FUTURE POSSIBILITIES

"Will" and "won't" describe things that are certain to happen or certain not to happen. Use "might" to show that something is not certain.

Negative
I **won't have** a vacation. I don't have enough money.

Possible
I **might have** a vacation. I have some money.

Positive
I **will have** a vacation because I have lots of money.

41.2 FURTHER EXAMPLES "MIGHT" WITH FUTURE POSSIBILITIES

To form the negative, add "not" between "might" and the verb. In UK English, it can be shortened to "mightn't."

He **might not go** to Rome this year. He doesn't know yet.

I **might speak** English at the party tonight as there are British people coming.

TIP
"Might" isn't normally used in questions.

41.3 HOW TO FORM "MIGHT" WITH FUTURE POSSIBILITIES

SUBJECT	"MIGHT"	MAIN VERB	REST OF SENTENCE
I / You He / She / It We / They	might might not mightn't	have	a vacation.

As with all modal verbs, "might" doesn't change with the subject.

Use the base form of the main verb.

41.4 REWRITE THE SENTENCES, PUTTING THE WORDS IN THE CORRECT ORDER

She | to | might | party. | my | come

She might come to my party.

1. dad | My | me | give | some money. | might

_____

2. might | Helen | test. | driving | pass | her

_____

3. bar. | might | I | not | a chocolate | eat

_____

4. They | not | have | party. | a | might

_____

41.5 REWRITE THE HIGHLIGHTED PHRASES, CORRECTING THE ERRORS

Hi Bill,

I'm excited about our hiking trip on Saturday. It might rains in the afternoon so we wills go in the morning. I'll brings some water, but I willn't bring any food. We mights wanting to stop at one of the pubs on our walk. What do you think?

See you this weekend,

Matt

It might rain

1. _____

2. _____

3. _____

4. _____

41.6 FILL IN THE GAPS USING "WON'T," "MIGHT," AND "WILL"

NEGATIVE	POSSIBLE	POSITIVE
I won't buy a computer.	I might buy a computer.	I will buy a computer.
1. _____	_____	They will make dinner.
2. _____	He might be late again.	_____
3. You won't remember that.	_____	_____
4. _____	She might become a teacher.	_____
5. _____	_____	We will win the game!
6. The dog won't eat this food.	_____	_____

137

41.7 KEY LANGUAGE "MIGHT" WITH UNCERTAINTY

You can use other phrases along with "might" to emphasize that you are uncertain about something.

 I might go to town. I'm not sure.

I don't know. I might have more pizza.

🔊

Aa 41.8 MATCH THE QUESTIONS TO THE ANSWERS

When are you going to clean your room?

1 Where will you live next year?

2 What will you do before you start college?

3 How much money are you taking on vacation?

I don't know. I might live in Boston.

I might get a summer job. I'm not sure.

I might do it this afternoon. I'm not sure.

I'm not sure. I might take about $300.

🔊

41.9 LISTEN TO THE AUDIO AND ANSWER THE QUESTIONS

Will John go to work today?
Yes, he will. ☐
He might. ☑
No, he won't. ☐

1 Is Mel going to the party this evening?
Yes, she is. ☐
She might. ☐
No, she isn't. ☐

2 Are Donna and Elise going swimming today?
Yes, they are. ☐
They might. ☐
No, they're not. ☐

3 Will Elliot be late for the concert?
Yes, he will. ☐
He might. ☐
No, he won't. ☐

4 Will Elsa study English?
Yes, she will. ☐
She might. ☐
No, she won't. ☐

5 Will Delilah travel by bus today?
Yes, she will. ☐
She might. ☐
No, she won't. ☐

41.10 SAY THE SENTENCES OUT LOUD USING "WILL," "MIGHT," AND "WON'T"

	POSITIVE	POSSIBLE	NEGATIVE
ABAN	go on vacation this year	① learn French	② run a marathon
NADIYA	③ become a doctor	④ write a book	⑤ do a bungee jump
JACK	⑥ get a dog	⑦ buy a motorcycle	⑧ move house

Aban will go on vacation this year.

①

②

③

④

⑤

⑥

⑦

⑧

42 Giving advice

If someone has a problem, one of the ways that you can give advice is by using the modal verb "should."

- ⚙ **New language** "Should"
- **Aa Vocabulary** Advice
- 🧩 **New skill** Giving advice

42.1 KEY LANGUAGE "SHOULD" TO GIVE ADVICE

"Should" shows that you think this is the best thing to do.

It's very sunny. You should wear a hat.

"Should" comes before the advice.

42.2 FURTHER EXAMPLES "SHOULD" TO GIVE ADVICE

It might rain. You should take your umbrella.

For a negative, add "not" between "should" and the main verb.

There's ice on the roads. You should not drive tonight.

"Should not" can be shortened to "shouldn't."

You're sick. You shouldn't go to work today.

42.3 HOW TO FORM "SHOULD" TO GIVE ADVICE

SUBJECT	"SHOULD"	MAIN VERB	REST OF SENTENCE
You	should	wear	a hat.

"Should" is a modal verb, so it stays the same no matter what the subject is.

"Should" is followed by the base form of the verb.

42.4 REWRITE THE SENTENCES, CORRECTING THE ERRORS

Kim should arrives on time.
Kim should arrive on time.

1 You shouldn't opens this door.

2 She shoulds to play the guitar every day.

3 He shouldn't wears that tie with that shirt.

4 You should to take a tablet twice a day.

5 They shouldn't to rides their bikes here.

42.5 LOOK AT THE PICTURES AND CROSS OUT THE INCORRECT WORDS IN THE SENTENCES TO GIVE GOOD ADVICE

Kim ~~should~~ / should not try to get on the train.

1 We should / shouldn't swim at this beach.

2 People should / should not be quiet in the library.

3 Shoppers should / shouldn't email.

4 They should / should not walk on the ice.

5 You should / shouldn't drive too fast.

141

Aa 42.6 MATCH THE PROBLEMS TO THE ADVICE

My plants are dying.	You should sell some of them.
1 I've got too many clothes.	You should get more sleep.
2 I eat too much junk food.	You should eat more fruit.
3 I don't know my neighbors.	You should water them.
4 I feel tired all the time.	You should join a gym.
5 I need more exercise.	You should have a block party.
6 I'm so lonely.	You should go shopping.
7 I've nothing to wear tonight.	You should get a dog.

42.7 LISTEN TO THE AUDIO AND MARK THE CORRECT PIECE OF ADVICE FOR EACH PROBLEM

To get to work tomorrow, James should...
- **leave early** ☐
- **take the bus** ☐
- **walk.** ☑

3 Sheila's busy at work. Martin says she should...
- **go to bed later** ☐
- **work on the weekend** ☐
- **get up earlier.** ☐

1 On the trip, people should...
- **bring $10** ☐
- **complete a form** ☐
- **be on time.** ☐

4 Atif's sister thinks he should...
- **buy a new computer** ☐
- **use a friend's computer** ☐
- **write emails on his phone.** ☐

2 Maya says Matt should first...
- **clean up** ☐
- **finish his work** ☐
- **eat dinner.** ☐

5 In the exam, students should...
- **be quiet** ☐
- **read all the information** ☐
- **speak clearly.** ☐

42.8 SAY THE SENTENCES OUT LOUD, FILLING IN THE GAPS USING "SHOULD" OR "SHOULDN'T"

He ___*shouldn't*___ go climbing in the rain.

3 You _____ eat anything in a laboratory.

1 People _____ visit the library more often.

4 You _____ go through that blue door.

2 People _____ have a shower before swimming.

5 Students _____ speak during their exams.

42 ✓ CHECKLIST

 "Should" ☐   **Aa** Advice ☐   Giving advice ☐

143

43 Making suggestions

You can use the modal verb "could" to offer suggestions. "Could" is not as strong as "should." It communicates gentle advice.

⚙ **New language** "Could" for suggestions
Aa Vocabulary Advice
🧩 **New skill** Making suggestions

43.1 KEY LANGUAGE "COULD" FOR SUGGESTIONS

"Could" is often used to suggest a solution to a problem. It introduces possibilities but not preferences.

I hate my car!

Well, you could get a new one!

"Could" means that the action is a possibility; a choice that might solve the problem.

🔊

43.2 FURTHER EXAMPLES "COULD" FOR SUGGESTIONS

You could study **science in college.**

We could learn **English in Canada next year.**

They could buy **a bigger house with a yard.**

You could get **a job at that new restaurant in town.**

🔊

43.3 HOW TO FORM "COULD" FOR SUGGESTIONS

SUBJECT	"COULD"	VERB	REST OF SENTENCE
You	could	get	a new car.

"Could" is a modal verb, so it doesn't change with the subject.

The main verb goes in its base form.

43.4 MATCH THE PROBLEMS TO THE CORRECT SUGGESTIONS

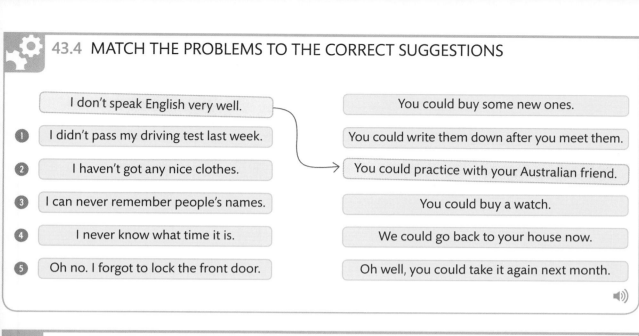

I don't speak English very well.

1 I didn't pass my driving test last week.

2 I haven't got any nice clothes.

3 I can never remember people's names.

4 I never know what time it is.

5 Oh no. I forgot to lock the front door.

You could buy some new ones.

You could write them down after you meet them.

You could practice with your Australian friend.

You could buy a watch.

We could go back to your house now.

Oh well, you could take it again next month.

43.5 CHOOSE THE CORRECT SUGGESTIONS FROM THE PANEL, THEN SAY THE SENTENCES OUT LOUD

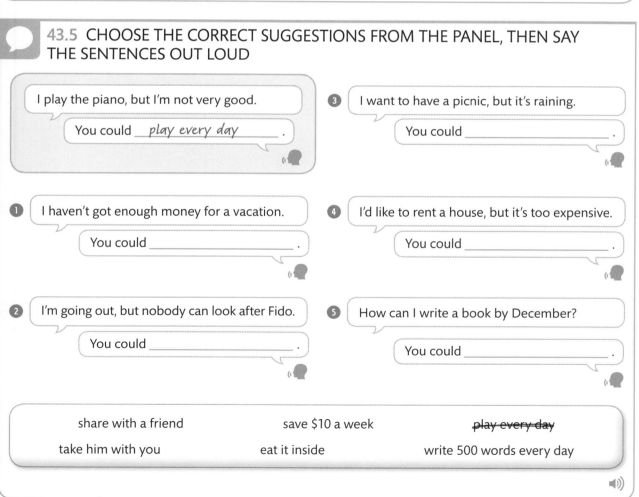

I play the piano, but I'm not very good.

You could _play every day_ .

3 I want to have a picnic, but it's raining.

You could _____ .

1 I haven't got enough money for a vacation.

You could _____ .

4 I'd like to rent a house, but it's too expensive.

You could _____ .

2 I'm going out, but nobody can look after Fido.

You could _____ .

5 How can I write a book by December?

You could _____ .

share with a friend   save $10 a week   play every day

take him with you   eat it inside   write 500 words every day

43.6 KEY LANGUAGE USING "COULD" AND "OR" FOR SUGGESTIONS

When people give suggestions using "could," they often give more than one option to choose from.

Our friends are coming over for dinner, but the oven's broken.

We could make a salad or we could order a pizza.

Use "or" to give an alternative suggestion.

43.7 FURTHER EXAMPLES USING "COULD" AND "OR" FOR SUGGESTIONS

I can't drive, but I want to travel along the coast.

You could take **a bus** or travel **in a friend's car.**

You don't have to repeat the modal verb "could" after "or."

What should I wear to Jan's wedding?

You could wear **your new dress** or a skir

If the main verb is the same for both suggestions, you don't repeat it after "or."

43.8 USE THE PHRASES TO WRITE SUGGESTIONS USING "COULD" AND "OR"

You can't sleep at night. You could _____read a book_____ or _____have a hot drink_____ .

1 You don't know what to do for the summer. You could _____ or _____ .

2 What are you going to make for dinner tonight? You could cook _____ or _____ .

3 You want to be a better tennis player. You could _____ or _____ .

4 You can't wake up in the mornings. You could _____ or _____ .

~~read a book~~   get a job   ~~have a hot drink~~   travel   chicken   set an alarm

have some lessons   go to bed earlier   beef   play more often

43.9 LISTEN TO THE AUDIO AND MARK THE TWO SUGGESTIONS GIVEN TO SOLVE EACH PROBLEM

Anya can't understand her English teacher very well. She could...
ask him to speak slowly. ☐ ask for notes on the lesson. ☑ record the lesson. ☑

1 Jim hasn't got time to do the chores at home. He could...
get his children to help. ☐ get a cleaner. ☐ not worry about it. ☐

2 Mandy needs to get a new job. She could...
look in the newspaper. ☐ ask friends. ☐ look at a website. ☐

3 Some students aren't very good at writing in English. They could...
read more English books. ☐ write in English every day. ☐ email a new friend in English. ☐

4 It's hard to find time to exercise. People could...
take the stairs. ☐ take the elevator. ☐ walk to the store. ☐

43 ✓ CHECKLIST

"Could" for suggestions ☐   Aa Advice ☐   Making suggestions ☐

↻ REVIEW THE ENGLISH YOU HAVE LEARNED IN UNITS 41–43

NEW LANGUAGE	SAMPLE SENTENCE	☑	UNIT
USING "MIGHT" WITH FUTURE POSSIBILITIES	I might have a vacation.	☐	41.1
USING "MIGHT" WITH UNCERTAINTY	I might go to town. I'm not sure. I don't know. I might have some pizza.	☐	41.7
USING "SHOULD" TO GIVE ADVICE	It's very sunny. You should wear a hat.	☐	42.1
USING "SHOULDN'T" TO GIVE ADVICE	You're sick. You shouldn't go to work today.	☐	42.2
USING "COULD" FOR SUGGESTIONS	You could get a new car.	☐	43.1
USING "OR" FOR SUGGESTIONS	We could make a salad or order a pizza.	☐	43.6

44.1 HOUSEHOLD CHORES

clean the windows

sweep the floor

scrub the floor

mop the floor

vacuum the carpet

dust

**take out the garbage (US)
take out the rubbish (UK)**

tidy

**go to the store (US)
go to the shops (UK)**

buy groceries

chop vegetables

cook dinner

set the table

clear the table

**do the dishes (US)
do the washing up (UK)**

dry the dishes

load the dishwasher

**do the laundry (US)
do the washing (UK)**

**hang clothes (US)
hang out the washing (UK)**

do the ironing

fold clothes

make the bed

change the sheets

do the gardening

mow the lawn

water the plants

wash the car

paint a room

hang a picture

walk the dog

feed the pets

mend the fence

45 Around the house

You can use the present perfect form of a verb to talk about something that has happened in the past and has consequences in the present.

⚙️ **New language** The present perfect
Aa Vocabulary Household chores
🧩 **New skill** Talking about the recent past

45.1 KEY LANGUAGE THE PRESENT PERFECT

Use the present perfect to describe something that has happened in the past and which has a result in the present moment.

TIP
Form regular past participles in the same way that you form the past simple, by adding "ed" to the base form of the verb.

"Just" means that the action has happened recently.

Tom has just cleaned the windows.

"Have" or "has" go after the subject in the present perfect.

The main verb goes in its past participle form.

🔊

45.2 FURTHER EXAMPLES THE PRESENT PERFECT

Look! I've just cooked **dinner.**

John has just washed **the dishes.**

You haven't cleared the table. It's a mess!

Have you cleaned up your bedroom?

 🔊

45.3 HOW TO FORM THE PRESENT PERFECT

SUBJECT + "HAVE" / "HAS"	"JUST"	PAST PARTICIPLE	OBJECT
I have	just	cleaned	the windows.

To make the present perfect, use "have" or "has" with the past participle of the verb.

45.4 KEY LANGUAGE FORMING IRREGULAR PAST PARTICIPLES

There are no rules for forming irregular past participles, but some irregular past participles have similar endings.

I am	➡	I've been
you eat	➡	you've eaten
they see	➡	they've seen
we do	➡	we've done
I put	➡	I've put
you leave	➡	you've left
they keep	➡	they've kept
we hear	➡	we've heard

◀))

45.5 FILL IN THE GAPS BY PUTTING THE VERBS INTO THE PRESENT PERFECT

I __have cleaned__ (clean) the kitchen.

1 We _____ (not mop) the floor.

2 Tim _____ (leave) the door open.

3 You _____ (change) the sheets.

4 Sheila _____ (eat) her dinner.

5 Dad _____ (not paint) the fence.

6 I _____ (vacuum) the living room.

7 Aziz _____ (water) the plants.

◀))

45.6 FILL IN THE GAPS TO WRITE EACH SENTENCE THREE DIFFERENT WAYS

He has washed his clothes.	He hasn't washed his clothes.	_Has he washed his clothes?_
1 They have cleaned the car.		
2		Have you mopped the floor?
3	I haven't taken the garbage out.	
4 You have painted the house.		
5		Has John cooked dinner?

Aa 45.7 FIND EIGHT REGULAR AND IRREGULAR PAST PARTICIPLES AND WRITE THEM NEXT TO THE CORRECT VERBS

```
C  L  E  A  T  E  N  N  E  N  H  L
L  V  P  C  H  A  D  U  W  Z  S  N
O  Q  D  O  N  E  P  Y  T  I  E  S
S  B  Z  K  Y  A  X (G  O  N  E) F
E  H  Q  L  X  G  J  A  T  D  N  K
D  E  B  E  E  N  S  E  H  A  K  E
K  A  G  Y  H  T  F  L  Z  J  K  J
E  D  W  T  N  G  K  E  P  T  Z  L
```

① go = _gone_

② have = _____

③ close = _____

④ eat = _____

⑤ am = _____

⑥ keep = _____

⑦ see = _____

⑧ do = _____

45.8 REWRITE THE SENTENCES, CORRECTING THE ERRORS

> Ellen **have** left her keys at home.
> _Ellen has left her keys at home._

① We have **cook** dinner for you.

_____

② Ben and Ellen **has** gone to the supermarket.

_____

③ The children have **see** the movie.

_____

④ Sheila has **clean** the bathroom.

_____

⑤ The dog **haven't** eaten all its food.

_____

⑥ They've **be** to the mall to buy you a present.

_____

45.9 LISTEN TO THE AUDIO AND ANSWER THE QUESTIONS

Adam and Becky are getting ready to have a party.

> Has Adam cleaned the bathroom?
> **Yes, he has.** ☑   **No, he hasn't.** ☐

① Have they bought enough drinks?
Yes, they have. ☐   **No, they haven't.** ☐

② Has Becky put the chicken in the oven?
Yes, she has. ☐   **No, she hasn't.** ☐

③ Has Adam talked to his sister?
Yes, he has. ☐   **No, he hasn't.** ☐

④ Has Adam's sister sent him a present?
Yes, she has. ☐   **No, she hasn't.** ☐

⑤ Has Adam moved his car?
Yes, he has. ☐   **No, he hasn't.** ☐

45.10 REWRITE THESE VERBS AS PAST PARTICIPLES

tidy = *tidied*

1 clean = _____

2 wash = _____

3 cook = _____

4 change = _____

5 mop = _____

6 walk = _____

7 clear = _____

8 brush = _____

45.11 SAY THE SENTENCES OUT LOUD, FILLING IN THE GAPS BY PUTTING THE VERBS FROM THE PANEL IN THE PRESENT PERFECT

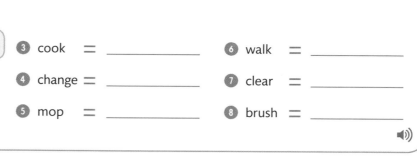

Mark has *washed* the dishes.

The children have _____ the car.

The cat has _____ all its food.

Jemma has _____ the window.

Jill has _____ her desk.

Paul has _____ his wallet on top of the car.

clean   wash   tidy   break   leave   eat

45 ✓ CHECKLIST

 The present perfect ☐   **Aa** Household chores ☐   Talking about the recent past ☐

153

46 Events in your life

Both the present perfect and the past simple can be used to talk about things that happened in the past, but you use them differently.

ϕ° New language The present perfect
Aa Vocabulary Adventure sports
New skill Talking about past events

46.1 KEY LANGUAGE THE PRESENT PERFECT AND THE PAST SIMPLE

Use the past simple to talk about something that happened at a definite time. Use the present perfect when you don't specify a particular time.

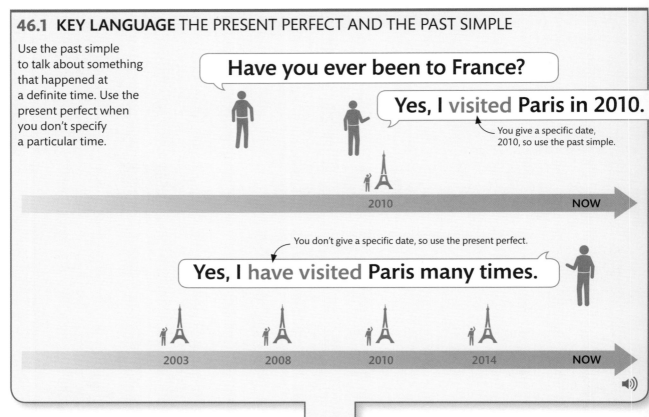

Have you ever been to France?

Yes, I visited Paris in 2010.

You give a specific date, 2010, so use the past simple.

2010 — NOW

You don't give a specific date, so use the present perfect.

Yes, I have visited Paris many times.

2003   2008   2010   2014   NOW

46.2 FURTHER EXAMPLES THE PRESENT PERFECT AND THE PAST SIMPLE

PAST SIMPLE	PRESENT PERFECT
I saw a great movie last week.	I haven't seen that movie.
Jo didn't climb Mount Fuji last year.	Saki has climbed Mount Fuji twice.
Madison ate too much last night.	Jack hasn't eaten curry before.

46.3 VOCABULARY ADVENTURE SPORTS

scuba diving	rock climbing	paragliding	windsurfing	bungee jumping	surfing

46.4 CROSS OUT THE INCORRECT WORDS IN EACH SENTENCE

Natalia **visited** / ~~has visited~~ China last year.

1 I love the movie *Casablanca*. I **watched** / **have watched** it more than nine times.

2 Our dog Rex **ate** / **has eaten** all Mary's birthday cake last night.

3 Jack **didn't visit** / **hasn't visited** the Colosseum when we were in Rome last year. He was too sick.

4 **Did you go** / **Have you been** to the swimming pool downtown yesterday?

46.5 SAY THE SENTENCES OUT LOUD, FILLING IN THE GAPS

Have you ever been surfing?

Yes, _I've been surfing_ many times.

3 Have you ever seen *Gone with the Wind*?

Yes, _____ last night.

1 Has Chloe ever been bungee jumping?

Yes, _____ many times.

4 Have you ever been paragliding?

No, _____ .

2 Has Liam ever visited Yosemite National Park?

Yes, _____ in 2014.

5 Have any of your friends been scuba diving?

Yes, Mia _____ many times.

46.6 KEY LANGUAGE "BEEN / GONE"

You can use "be" and "go" in the present perfect to talk about your trips to places, but they have different meanings.

I haven't seen Joan recently. Where is she?

She's gone to Florida.

She is still in Florida.

Hi, Joan. You're looking well.

Yes, I've been to Florida.

She went to Florida, but now she is back home.

46.7 FURTHER EXAMPLES "BEEN / GONE"

Where's Ben?

He's gone to the mall.

Where's Ariana?

She's gone windsurfing.

You look relaxed.

Yes, we've been in Bermuda. We had a great time.

What's Julie doing?

She's been swimming and now she's doing her homework.

46.8 FILL IN THE GAPS USING "BEEN" OR "GONE"

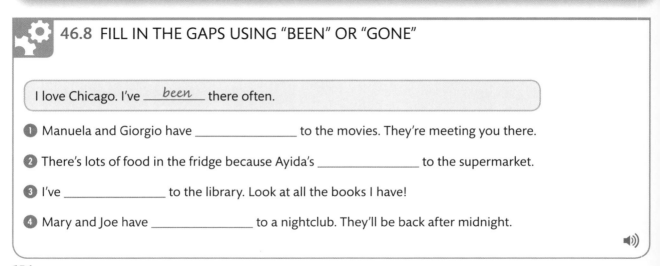

I love Chicago. I've ___been___ there often.

1 Manuela and Giorgio have _____ to the movies. They're meeting you there.

2 There's lots of food in the fridge because Ayida's _____ to the supermarket.

3 I've _____ to the library. Look at all the books I have!

4 Mary and Joe have _____ to a nightclub. They'll be back after midnight.

46.9 READ THE POSTCARD AND WRITE THE VERBS UNDER THE CORRECT HEADINGS

PRESENT PERFECT

we've seen

1. _____

2. _____

PAST SIMPLE

we got

3. _____

4. _____

Hi Chris,
We're in Sydney! We got here five days ago and we've seen so much. On Monday, we visited the Sydney Opera House, and on Tuesday we went on a boat under Harbour Bridge. We haven't been to Bondi Beach yet, but I think we're going tomorrow. We've eaten some great food, too! Wish you were here.
Love,
Olivia x

46.10 LISTEN TO THE AUDIO AND ANSWER THE QUESTIONS

Martin has been bungee jumping three times.
True ☐ **False** ☑

1. Sammy went to China in 2011.
True ☐ **False** ☐

2. Nigel has never cooked a meal for visitors.
True ☐ **False** ☐

3. Debra has been rock climbing many times.
True ☐ **False** ☐

4. Andrew has never used a tablet before.
True ☐ **False** ☐

46.11 REWRITE THE SENTENCES, CORRECTING THE ERRORS

I've **gone** windsurfing many times.
I've been windsurfing many times.

1. She hasn't **be** to the circus.

_____

2. I **meet** my best friend when I was six.

_____

3. You **eat** all the chocolate last night.

_____

4. He hasn't **try** paragliding.

_____

46 ✓ CHECKLIST

⚙ The present perfect ☐   **Aa** Adventure sports ☐   🧩 Talking about past events ☐

47 Events in your year

One of the uses of the present perfect is to talk about events in a time period that hasn't finished. Use the past simple for a time period that is completed.

⚙ **New language** "Yet" and "already"
Aa Vocabulary Routines and chores
🧩 **New skill** Talking about the recent past

47.1 KEY LANGUAGE PRESENT PERFECT AND PAST SIMPLE

If the time period referred to is ongoing, use the present perfect. Use the past simple to talk about a completed event.

This year has not finished yet. Use the present perfect.

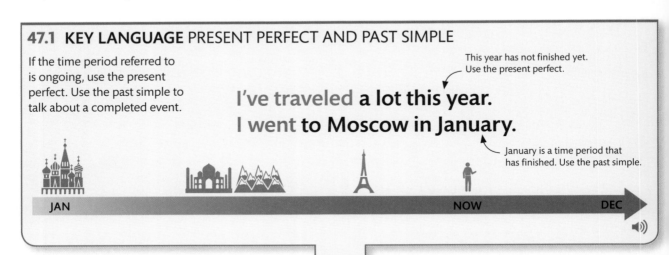

I've traveled a lot this year.
I went to Moscow in January.

January is a time period that has finished. Use the past simple.

JAN   NOW   DEC

47.2 FURTHER EXAMPLES PRESENT PERFECT AND PAST SIMPLE

 I haven't had **any coffee this morning.**

 The photocopier **broke yesterday.**

 I've had **a lot of meetings today.**

 My manager **called me last night.**

47.3 FILL IN THE GAPS BY PUTTING THE VERBS IN THE PRESENT PERFECT OR PAST SIMPLE

I'm flying to New York again tomorrow. I ___*have been*___ (be) there five times this year.

1 Alvita is very happy. She _____ (win) the prize for the best chocolate cake yesterday.

2 This is a great party. I _____ (meet) lots of really fun and interesting people.

3 Martha looks happy. She _____ (be) to the movies with Miles.

4 Mary can't drive. She _____ (fall) and _____ (break) her arm last week.

TENNIS STAR'S DIFFICULT YEAR

Sarah Jackson speaks to our sports reporter.

Sarah Jackson is a tennis player from the US. She has won five tennis championships, but she hasn't played in any competitions this year.

"I haven't had a good year. I broke my leg in January and I didn't play tennis for three months. It was really painful and it took me a long time to get well."

There are four big competitions for tennis players, known as the Grand Slams: the Australian Open, the French Open, Wimbledon, and the US Open. Sarah has already missed two of them.

"It's difficult for tennis players. You want to do well in the big competitions, but sometimes you can't."

The next grand slam is Wimbledon, but Sarah isn't going to play this year. "It's sad, but I'm just not ready for Wimbledon at the moment."

But the year hasn't been all bad: "I don't usually go on vacation," she told us, "but in March I went to the Caribbean. I had a really good time and relaxed. I also ate some great food and went swimming."

How many tennis championships has Sarah won?

She has won five tennis championships.

❸ How long didn't she play tennis for?

❶ What hasn't Sarah done this year?

❹ How many grand slams has Sarah missed this year?

❷ What did Sarah do in January?

❺ What did Sarah do in March this year?

47.5 KEY LANGUAGE "YET"

"Yet" means "until now." It shows that you have an intention to do something.

Have you ordered the pizzas?

No, I haven't ordered them yet.

You haven't ordered the pizzas, but you will order them later.

47.6 KEY LANGUAGE "ALREADY"

Use "already" when something has happened, possibly sooner than expected.

I'll order the pizzas now.

It's OK. I've already ordered them.

You've ordered the pizzas before the other person expected.

47.7 FURTHER EXAMPLES "ALREADY" AND "YET"

Has Rob cooked the dinner?

No, not yet.

You can use "yet" in short answers.

What time is Andrew going to get here?

He's already arrived.

47.8 MATCH THE QUESTIONS TO THE CORRECT ANSWERS

When is Phil going to get here?

No, the game hasn't started yet.

1 Am I too late to play football?

I've already done it.

2 Has Amy learned how to drive yet?

He's already arrived.

3 Can you send an email to Rachel?

No, not yet.

4 Have you watched this movie?

Yes, I've already seen it.

Sharon and Paul are getting ready to leave home and go on vacation.

Paul hasn't booked a taxi yet.
True ☐ **False** ☑

① Paul hasn't made the sandwiches yet.
True ☐ **False** ☐

② Sharon has already called her mother.
True ☐ **False** ☐

③ Sharon hasn't checked if the dog is OK yet.
True ☐ **False** ☐

④ The dog has already been for a walk.
True ☐ **False** ☐

⑤ Sharon has already mailed her letter.
True ☐ **False** ☐

47.10 LOOK AT SANTIAGO'S "TO DO" LIST AND WRITE ANSWERS TO THE QUESTIONS AS FULL SENTENCES USING "ALREADY" AND "YET"

Has Santiago fed the cat yet?
Yes, he's already fed the cat.

Has he put out the garbage yet?
No, he hasn't put out the garbage yet.

To do list

~~Feed the cat~~
Put out the garbage
~~Clean the kitchen~~
~~Buy milk and bread~~
~~Mail letter~~
Make birthday cake
Call Grandma
Take dog for walk

① Has he cleaned the kitchen yet?

_____

② Has he bought milk and bread yet?

_____

③ Has he taken the dog for a walk yet?

_____

④ Has he made the birthday cake yet?

_____

⑤ Has he mailed the letter yet?

_____

⑥ Has he called his grandmother yet?

_____

47 ✓ CHECKLIST

⚙ "Yet" and "already" ☐   **Aa** Routines and chores ☐   Talking about the recent past ☐

48 Eating out

"Eating out" means having a meal outside your home, usually in a restaurant. To do this, you need to know the language for making a reservation and ordering food.

🪛 **New language** Restaurant phrases
Aa Vocabulary Food preparation
🧩 **New skill** Ordering a meal in a restaurant

48.1 KEY LANGUAGE ORDERING A MEAL

A restaurant meal often has three courses.

Have you made a reservation?

Yes, we have.

Would you like to see the menu?

Yes, please.

Are you ready to order?

Could we have a few more minutes?

For my main course, I'd like the fish. And for dessert, I'll have the apple pie.

TIP
In US English, you can use "entrée" or "main course" to describe the main dish in a meal.

How's your meal?

It's delicious, thank you.

Excuse me! Can we have the check, please?

Of course, sir.

48.2 VOCABULARY EATING OUT AND FOOD PREPARATION

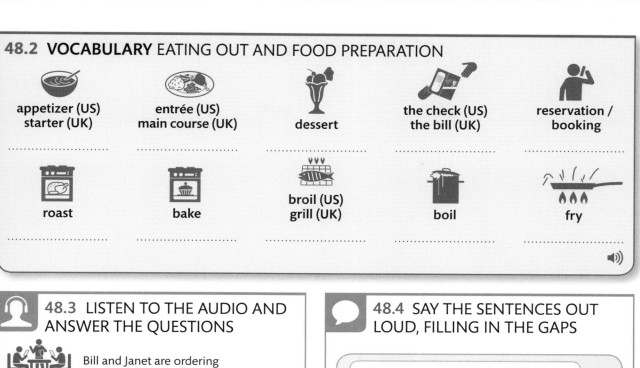

appetizer (US)
starter (UK)

entrée (US)
main course (UK)

dessert

the check (US)
the bill (UK)

reservation /
booking

roast

bake

broil (US)
grill (UK)

boil

fry

48.3 LISTEN TO THE AUDIO AND ANSWER THE QUESTIONS

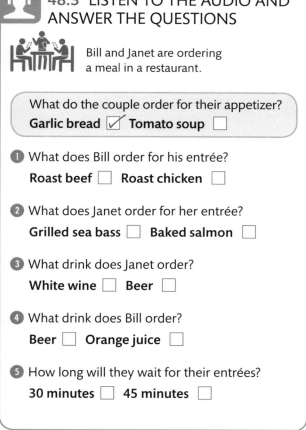

Bill and Janet are ordering
a meal in a restaurant.

What do the couple order for their appetizer?
Garlic bread ☑ **Tomato soup** ☐

1 What does Bill order for his entrée?
Roast beef ☐ **Roast chicken** ☐

2 What does Janet order for her entrée?
Grilled sea bass ☐ **Baked salmon** ☐

3 What drink does Janet order?
White wine ☐ **Beer** ☐

4 What drink does Bill order?
Beer ☐ **Orange juice** ☐

5 How long will they wait for their entrées?
30 minutes ☐ **45 minutes** ☐

48.4 SAY THE SENTENCES OUT LOUD, FILLING IN THE GAPS

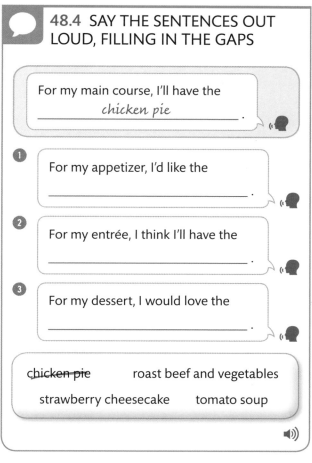

For my main course, I'll have the
_chicken pie_____ .

1 For my appetizer, I'd like the
_____ .

2 For my entrée, I think I'll have the
_____ .

3 For my dessert, I would love the
_____ .

~~chicken pie~~   roast beef and vegetables

strawberry cheesecake   tomato soup

48 ✓ CHECKLIST

⚙ Restaurant phrases ☐   **Aa** Food preparation ☐   🧩 Ordering a meal in a restaurant ☐

49 Achievements and ambitions

English uses different phrases to talk about future wishes
or desires, definite future plans, and past achievements.
Use them in conversation to talk about your life.

🔧 **New language** Desires and plans
Aa Vocabulary Travel and adventure sports
🧩 **New skill** Talking about your achievements

49.1 KEY LANGUAGE DESIRES AND PLANS

Use expressions
such as "I'd like to"
for desires. Use
"I'm going to"
for definite plans.

Have you ever worked abroad?

You want to work abroad.

No, but I'd like to work in Asia.

No, but I'm going to next year.

Your plan is to work
abroad next year.

🔊

49.2 FURTHER EXAMPLES DESIRES AND PLANS

I'm very excited. We're going to
hike the Inca Trail next year.

I haven't climbed Mount Fuji,
but I'm going to do it this summer.

I've never been to South America,
but I want to go.

I've never seen a whale. I'd like to
go whale-watching later this year.

🔊

49.3 MATCH THE QUESTIONS TO THE CORRECT ANSWERS

Have you ever played golf?

1 Have you ever been paragliding?

2 Have you ever seen *Hamlet*?

3 Have you ever been to Machu Picchu?

4 Have you ever been on a boat?

No, but I love Shakespeare and I'd like to see it.

No, but I want to do that next year.

No, but I'm going to watch the US Open.

No, but I want to go sailing in the summer.

No, but we're going to go there next year.

🔊

49.4 LISTEN TO THE AUDIO AND MARK WHAT BRETT HAS OR HASN'T DONE

Radio presenter Ken Wallace interviews stunt man Brett Ellis.

Has done ✓   Hasn't done ☐

1 Has done ☐   Hasn't done ☐

2 Has done ☐   Hasn't done ☐

3 Has done ☐   Hasn't done ☐

Aa 49.5 READ THE CLUES AND WRITE THE ANSWERS IN THE CORRECT PLACES ON THE GRID

| | ¹D | e | s | ²e | r | t |

ACROSS

1 Davina is going to ride a camel across the Gobi _____Desert_____ .

3 Harry wants to _____ along the Pacific Coast Highway.

6 Dan would like to go swimming with _____ in Mexico.

7 Flo would like to study _____ in Beijing.

9 Susie wants to see kangaroos in _____ .

DOWN

2 Javier wants to speak _____ every day.

4 Ben would like to climb a _____ .

5 José wants to play _____ with the Dallas Cowboys.

8 Gary is going to _____ a short movie with his friends.

10 Melinda wants to _____ her boat around the world.

| ~~Desert~~ | sail | dolphins | Australia | drive |
| football | Chinese | make | mountain | English |

49.6 KEY LANGUAGE THINGS I'VE DONE AND WANT TO DO

Use words such as "never," "yet," or "really" to place a different emphasis on what you're saying.

I've **never** run a marathon.

"I've never ..." is stronger than "I've not ..."

I haven't seen the Pyramids of Giza **yet**.

You haven't seen the Pyramids of Giza until now, but you intend to see them one day.

I **really** want to climb Mount Everest.

Your desire to climb Mount Everest is strong.

🔊

Aa 49.7 MATCH THE PICTURES TO THE CORRECT SENTENCES

I haven't been up in a hot-air balloon, but I'm going to do that for my birthday in August.

I haven't traveled in a helicopter yet, but I'm going to fly over New York in one soon.

①

I haven't been to a music festival yet, but my friends really want to take me to one next summer.

②

I've never learned to ski, but my friend Sanjay is going to teach me next year.

③

I've never been on TV, but I'm going to be on a TV quiz show in a few weeks. I'm very excited.

④

🔊

49.8 READ THE EMAIL AND ANSWER THE QUESTIONS

John has been surfing in South Africa and Australia.
True ☐ **False** ☑

① John has never seen a lion.
True ☐ **False** ☐

② John and Jo have been on safari before.
True ☐ **False** ☐

③ John and Jo are going to China this year.
True ☐ **False** ☐

④ John wants to go to Japan this summer.
True ☐ **False** ☐

⑤ Jo has never been on an elephant.
True ☐ **False** ☐

✉

To: Jo Abernathy

Subject: Things I want to do this year

Hi Jo,
I want to plan our year, so we can do more things. We've already been surfing in Australia and Hawaii, but we haven't surfed in South Africa yet. I've also never seen a lion, so I want to go on safari. We've never done that before. Also, I know we're going to China next year, but this summer I want to go to Thailand. I'd really like to ride an elephant, and I know you haven't done that yet. What do you think?
John

49 ✓ CHECKLIST

⚙ Desires and plans ☐   **Aa** Travel and adventure sports ☐   🧩 Talking about your achievements ☐

↻ REVIEW THE ENGLISH YOU HAVE LEARNED IN UNITS 45-49

NEW LANGUAGE	SAMPLE SENTENCE	☑	UNIT
THE PRESENT PERFECT	Tom has just cleaned the windows.	☐	45.1, 45.3
THE PAST SIMPLE AND THE PRESENT PERFECT	I visited France in 2010. I have visited France many times.	☐	46.1
"YET" AND "ALREADY" WITH THE PRESENT PERFECT	I haven't ordered the pizza yet. I've already ordered the pizza.	☐	47.5, 47.6
ORDERING A MEAL	"Have you made a reservation?" "Yes, I have." "Excuse me! Can we have the check, please."	☐	48.1
DESIRES AND PLANS	I'd like to work in Asia. I'm going to work there next year.	☐	49.1, 49.2, 49.6

R Reference

R1 ADJECTIVES

An **adjective** is used to describe the qualities of a noun. It usually comes before the noun that it is describing. Some adjectives have irregular comparative and superlative forms.

A **comparative adjective** is used to describe the difference between two things. Use it before the word "than" to compare people, places, or things. If an adjective is three syllables or longer, use "more" or "less" before the adjective and "than" after it.

A **superlative adjective** is used to talk about extremes, or to describe a person or thing that possesses a certain quality more than anyone or anything else. For long adjectives, add "the most" or "the least" before the adjective to make the superlative.

ADJECTIVE	COMPARATIVE	SUPERLATIVE	ADJECTIVE	COMPARATIVE	SUPERLATIVE
angry	angrier	angriest	heavy	heavier	heaviest
bad	**worse**	**worst**	high	higher	highest
beautiful	beautiful	beautiful	horrible	horrible	horrible
big	bigger	biggest	hot	hotter	hottest
busy	busier	busiest	important	important	important
cheap	cheaper	cheapest	interesting	interesting	interesting
clean	cleaner	cleanest	large	larger	largest
close	closer	closest	late	later	latest
cold	colder	coldest	long	longer	longest
dangerous	dangerous	dangerous	lucky	luckier	luckiest
deep	deeper	deepest	new	newer	newest
difficult	difficult	difficult	nice	nicer	nicest
early	earlier	earliest	noisy	noisier	nosiest
easy	easier	easiest	old	older	oldest
exciting	exciting	exciting	pretty	prettier	prettiest
expensive	expensive	expensive	quiet	quieter	quietest
far	farther (US)	farthest (US)	sad	sadder	saddest
	further (UK)	**furthest** (UK)	safe	safer	safest
fast	faster	fastest	simple	simpler	simplest
few	fewer	fewest	short	shorter	shortest
friendly	friendlier	friendliest	small	smaller	smallest
good	**better**	**best**	tall	taller	tallest
happy	happier	happiest	warm	warmer	warmest
hard	harder	hardest	young	younger	youngest

R2   COMMON STATE VERBS

State verbs are usually used to express a state of being, i.e. to say how things are or how someone feels. They can be used to talk about emotions, possession, senses, or thoughts. They are not usually used in continuous tenses.

MEANING	STATE VERB	SAMPLE SENTENCE
feeling / wanting	**like / love**	I **like / love** Italian ice cream.
	need	We really **need** to spend more time together as a family.
	prefer	Some people **prefer** summer to winter.
	want	The band **wants** to become famous and make money.
thinking	**believe**	I **believe** your story, but it is rather unlikely.
	doubt	Lots of people **doubt** that he can do the job properly.
	know	Do you **know** where we parked the car?
	mean	What do you **mean** when you say you aren't ready?
	think	What do you **think** about the proposed policy?
	understand	Could you speak more slowly? I don't **understand** you.
being / existing	**appear / seem**	It **appears / seems** that the house has already been sold.
	exist	Strange creatures **exist** at the bottom of the sea.
possessing	**belong**	Excuse me, that book **belongs** to me.
	have / own	My cousin **has / owns** three classic cars.
	include	Did you **include** Lucy in the guest list?
sensing	**feel**	Does your leg **feel** better today?
	hear	I can **hear** you, but I'm not sure what you're saying.
	hurt	My arm really **hurts**. I think I should go to see the doctor.
	see	Can you **see** the blackbird in the bush over there?
having a quality	**feel**	This rug **feels** so soft. It would be lovely to walk on.
	smell	Something **smells** delicious. Is it the soup?
	sound	That **sounds** like thunder, or is it just fireworks?
	taste	This milk **tastes** a bit sour. I think it's gone bad.

169

R3 MODAL VERBS

Modal verbs modify the meaning of the main verb, expressing various notions such as possibility or obligation. They don't change form to match the subject, and they are always followed by a main verb in its base form.

CAN

"Can" can be used to describe what someone or something is able to do. It can also be used to ask permission or make a request.

SUBJECT	"CAN"	MAIN VERB	REST OF SENTENCE
I You He / She / It We You They	can cannot can't	play	tennis.

COULD

"Could" can be used in a variety of ways. It can be used to describe what something or someone was able to do in the past. It can also be used to make a polite request, offer a suggestion or solution, or ask for permission. It introduces possibilities but not preferences. It is not as strong as "should".

SUBJECT	"COULD"	MAIN VERB	REST OF SENTENCE
I You He / She / It We You They	could could not couldn't	buy	a new car.

MIGHT

"Might" can be used to talk about something that a person may or not do in the future.
It can also be used to express uncertainty. It is only a possibility and not an assertion.

SUBJECT	"MIGHT"	MAIN VERB	REST OF SENTENCE
I You He / She / It We You They	might might not mightn't	come	**to the party.**

SHOULD

"Should" can be used to give advice. It can also be used to
state what you expect will happen.

SUBJECT	"SHOULD"	MAIN VERB	REST OF SENTENCE
I You He / She / It We You They	should should not shouldn't	visit	**the museum.**

WOULD

"Would" can be used to express something that someone wants to do.
It can also be used to describe what someone used to do in the past.

SUBJECT	"WOULD"	MAIN VERB	REST OF SENTENCE
I You He / She / It We You They	would would not wouldn't	like	**to travel abroad.**

THE PRESENT CONTINUOUS

The **present continuous** is used to talk about something that is happening **now** in the present moment. There are no irregular verb forms in the present continuous. Note that state verbs are not usually used in continuous tenses.

POSITIVE	NEGATIVE	QUESTION
I am / I'm talking	I'm not talking	Am I talking...?
You are / You're talking	You're not / You aren't talking	Are you talking...?
He is / He's talking	He's not / He isn't talking	Is he talking...?
She is / She's talking	She's not / She isn't talking	Is she talking...?
It is / It's talking	It's not / It isn't talking	Is it talking...?
We are / We're talking	We're not / We aren't talking	Are we talking...?
You are / You're talking	You're not / You aren't talking	Are you talking...?
They are / They're talking	They're not / They aren't talking	Are they talking...?

R5 **THE PRESENT PERFECT: REGULAR VERBS**

The **present perfect** is used to talk about events in the past that have an effect on the present moment. It is formed using the verb **"to have"** plus the past participle of the verb that describes the event. See R10 for a list of irregular past participles.

POSITIVE	NEGATIVE	QUESTION
I have / I've helped	I've not / I haven't helped	Have I helped...?
You have / You've helped	You've not / You haven't helped	Have you helped...?
He has / He's helped	He's not / He hasn't helped	Has he helped...?
She has / She's helped	She's not / She hasn't helped	Has she helped...?
It has / It's helped	It's not / It hasn't helped	Has it helped...?
We have / We've helped	We've not / We haven't helped	Have we helped...?
You have / You've helped	You've not / You haven't helped	Have you helped...?
They have / They've helped	They've not / They haven't helped	Have they helped...?

R6 THE FUTURE WITH "GOING TO"

When discussing the future, **"going to"** is used to talk about decisions that have already been made, or to make predictions when there is evidence in the present moment to support them.

POSITIVE	NEGATIVE	QUESTION
I am / I'm going to	I'm not going to	Am I going to...?
You are / You're going to	You're not / You aren't going to	Are you going to...?
He is / He's going to	He's not / He isn't going to	Is he going to...?
She is / She's going to	She's not / She isn't going to	Is she going to...?
It is / It's going to	It's not / It isn't going to	Is it going to...?
We are / We're going to	We're not / We aren't going to	Are we going to...?
You are / You're going to	You're not / You aren't going to	Are you going to...?
They are / They're going to	They're not / They aren't going to	Are they going to...?

R7 THE FUTURE WITH "WILL"

When discussing the future, **"will"** is used to talk about decisions made at the time of speaking, to make predictions about the future that are not supported by evidence, to offer to do something, or to make promises.

POSITIVE	NEGATIVE	QUESTION
I will / I'll	I will not / I won't	Will I...?
You will / You'll	You will not / You won't	Will you...?
He will / He'll	He will not / He won't	Will he...?
She will / She'll	She will not / She won't	Will she...?
It will / It'll	It will not / It won't	Will it..?
We will / We'll	We will not / We won't	Will we...?
You will / You'll	You will not / You won't	Will you...?
They will / They'll	They will not / They won't	Will they...?

R8 THE PAST SIMPLE: REGULAR VERBS

The **past simple** is used to describe events that happened at a definite time in the past, or to describe the state of things at a particular point in time. It is used to refer to completed actions in the past. The past simple forms of regular verbs usually end in "-ed".

POSITIVE	NEGATIVE	QUESTION
I worked	I did not / I didn't work	Did I work...?
You worked	You did not / You didn't work	Did you work...?
He worked	He did not / He didn't work	Did he work...?
She worked	She did not / She didn't work	Did she work...?
It worked	It did not / It didn't work	Did it work...?
We worked	We did not / We didn't work	Did we work...?
You worked	You did not / You didn't work	Did you work...?
They worked	They did not / They didn't work	Did they work...?

R9 THE PAST SIMPLE: "TO BE"

The **past simple** form of **"to be"** is completely irregular. It is the only verb in the past simple which changes depending on the subject.

POSITIVE	NEGATIVE	QUESTION
I was	I was not / I wasn't	Was I...?
You were	You were not / You weren't	Were you...?
He was	He was not / He wasn't	Was he...?
She was	She was not / She wasn't	Was she...?
It was	It was not / It wasn't	Was it...?
We were	We were not / We weren't	Were we...?
You were	You were not / You weren't	Were you...?
They were	They were not / They weren't	Were they...?

R10   THE PAST SIMPLE AND PAST PARTICIPLE: IRREGULAR VERBS

Some verbs have irregular forms for the **past simple** tense and the **past participle**.
The tables below list some of the most common.

BASE FORM	PAST SIMPLE	PAST PARTICIPLE	BASE FORM	PAST SIMPLE	PAST PARTICIPLE
be	was / were	been	leave	left	left
begin	began	begun	lose	lost	lost
break	broke	broken	make	made	made
bring	brought	brought	mean	meant	meant
build	built	built	meet	met	met
buy	bought	bought	put	put	put
catch	caught	caught	read	read	read
choose	chose	chosen	ride	rode	rode
come	came	come	ring	rang	rung
cost	cost	cost	run	ran	run
cut	cut	cut	say	said	said
do	did	done	see	saw	seen
draw	drew	drawn	send	sent	sent
drink	drank	drunk	sit	sat	sat
drive	drove	driven	sell	sold	sold
eat	ate	eaten	show	showed	shown
fall	fell	fallen	shut	shut	shut
fight	fought	fought	sleep	slept	slept
find	found	found	speak	spoke	spoken
fly	flew	flown	sing	sang	sung
forget	forgot	forgotten	spend	spent	spent
freeze	froze	frozen	stand	stood	stood
get	got	gotten (US) / got (UK)	steal	stole	stolen
give	gave	given	swim	swam	swum
go	went	gone	swing	swung	swung
grow	grew	grown	take	took	taken
hear	heard	heard	teach	taught	taught
have	had	had	tell	told	told
hit	hit	hit	think	thought	thought
hold	held	held	throw	threw	thrown
hurt	hurt	hurt	understand	understood	understood
keep	kept	kept	wear	wore	worn
know	knew	known	win	won	won
lend	lent	lent	write	wrote	written

Transcripts of listening exercises

UNIT 1

1.6 ex: Hi. I'm Charlie and I am a doctor.
1.6.1 Hello, my name's Altan. I am American.
1.6.2 Hi, I'm Latifa. I'm an engineer.
1.6.3 My name's Ollie. I'm British and I'm 26 years old.
1.6.4 My name's Kathleen. I am a chef and I'm from Australia.
1.6.5 I'm Sammi. I'm 46 years old and I'm a vet.

UNIT 3

3.6

Friend: I like this photo of your family, Emma. You all look great!
Emma: Thanks. That's my dad beside me. He is wearing a wonderful gray suit and his favorite tie. I'm wearing my red dress and my favorite hat.
Friend: Is that your older brother?
Emma: Yes, that's Max. He loves that suit and that silly hat.
Friend: He looks funny. And that's Julie next to him, yeah?
Emma: Yes, she always wears jeans, but in this photo she's wearing her lovely blue skirt with a green jacket.
Friend: And she's beside your mother?
Emma: No, it's my cousin, Jada. She loves wearing strong colors.
Friend: I like her yellow jacket. It's very bright!
Emma: I know!

3.12

Friend: Hi Sam. It's very quiet in here. What are all your housemates doing?
Sam: Well, Ed's not watching TV. He's reading a book instead.
Friend: And what's Dan doing?
Sam: He's watching TV. There's a movie on now.
Friend: OK, and where's Manu? I can hear some music.
Sam: Actually, Manu's doing some exercise. The music is George playing his guitar. He's in a band.
Friend: Oh, that's great. And how about Jamal? Is he walking the dog?

Friend: He wanted to, but it's raining, so he's staying inside. I think he's playing a computer game.
Friend: Shall we join him?
Sam: Sure, let's ask him.

UNIT 4

4.5

Martha: Hi, Jack. It's Martha.
Jack: Oh, hi, Martha. How are you?
Martha: Great! How are you?
Jack: I'm fine. I'm relaxing in the yard at the moment. The sun is lovely today.
Martha: So nice that I'm gardening all day today! Is Rachel with you?
Jack: She's cooking in the kitchen.
Martha: Is Fleur helping her?
Jack: Not really. She's listening to music in her bedroom. She always does that on a Sunday afternoon. And Jacob's reading a book. He has a lot of work to do for university.
Martha: Well, say hi to everyone for me. And can you ask Rachel to call me later?
Jack: Sure.
Martha: We need to talk about...

4.9 ex: Friend: Hi, Jim! Is that your new tablet?
Jim: No, it's my smartphone.
Friend: Wow. It's big.
Jim: I know. I love it!
4.9.1
Friend: Hi, Lucas. What are you doing?
Lucas: Oh, it's silly. I'm cleaning my shirt. There's spaghetti on it!
4.9.2
Friend: Hi, Orla. Are you playing a game on your computer?
Orla: No, I'm doing some work on it.
4.9.3
Friend: Hi, Livia. Are you going out?
Livia: Yes.
Friend: You look nice. That's a lovely dress.
Livia: Oh, thanks. It's a skirt and top. It's my favorite outfit, actually.
4.9.4
Friend: Hi, David. What are you doing on your tablet?

David: I'm writing an email right now, but I do lots of things on it. I read books on it in the evening.
Friend: Oh, me too. I've got lots of books on mine.
4.9.5
Friend: Hi, Dewain. Have you got new headphones?
Dewain: Yep! Do you like them?
Friend: They're really nice ones. Are you listening to music?
Dewain: Not music, no. I'm listening to news on the radio.
4.9.6
Friend: Hi, Rochelle! Is that heavy? Can I help you carry it?
Rochelle: No, thanks. I'm fine. It's my new laptop. It's really light.
4.9.7
Friend: Hi, Julio. Is that a new tablet?
Julio: No, it's an e-reader. I'm reading a great book on it at the moment.

UNIT 7

7.6 ex: Jack: Oh, no. Where's my notes? My pen? I can't remember. Er... Ladies and gentlemen, welcome to... er... what's it called? Er... This building is... Help!
7.6.1
Jill: I'm great. Life's good at the moment. I've got a new job and a new boyfriend. And at the moment, I'm on holiday. Yay!
7.6.2
Sami: There's nothing on TV. No good movies to watch. No books to read. Nothing to do.
7.6.3
Ian: We're here on the Serengeti, waiting for the lions. They come here every day to drink at about midday, and here they come now.
7.6.4
Lindi: I can't believe it. Where are my keys? Where are they? I'm so late for work! Come on!
7.6.5
Jenny: It's our last exam. I'm so happy. I can't wait to finish my course.